My Life as a Diabetic

My Life as a Diabetic

Celeste Barnard

Copyright © 2019 by Celeste Barnard.

ISBN: 9781645501701

All rights reserved. No part of this book may be reproduced or transmitted in any form or by any means, electronic or mechanical, including photocopying, recording, or by any information storage and retrieval system, without permission in writing from the copyright owner.

Any people depicted in stock imagery provided by Getty Images are models, and such images are being used for illustrative purposes only.
Certain stock imagery © Getty Images.

CONTENTS

Introduction vii

Chapter 1	Discovering Diabetes 1
Chapter 2	The Beginning Stages Of Living My Life As A Diabetic 6
Chapter 3	Being Admitted Into The Hospital For The First Time 12
Chapter 4	Moving To A Warmer Part Of The Country 30
Chapter 5	My First Trip To And From South Africa 34
Chapter 6	Two Guardian Angels 55
Chapter 7	The Second Last Hurdle 64
Chapter 8	Just When I Thought That I Would Never See A Hospital Again 73
Chapter 9	Are You Kidding Me! 81
Chapter 10	How You Can Help Others From Your Own Experiences 88
Chapter 11	Some Scary Moments Many Years Ago 96
Chapter 12	People's Opinions Of Me As A Diabetic 108
Chapter 13	These Are The Things That I Keep In Mind Everyday 114

Chapter 14 Bedtime Story 119

Chapter 15 An Unexpected Change 122

Chapter 16 A Few Handy Hints 129

Summary 133

Index 135

INTRODUCTION

Hello, my name is Celeste Barnard. I would like to take you on the roller-coaster journey of my life as a **Type 1** diabetic (insulin dependent). As you read through my life experiences, I hope that you will find incidents you can relate to and that, in so doing, you will feel more comfortable and less frustrated with knowing that you are not alone on your sometimes difficult daily walk through life as a diabetic. I hope that by sharing some of my experiences with you, I will be able to help you answer some of the questions that you may have in regard to your own health issues. I do want to make it very clear, though, that I am not a medical practitioner, so whatever I state in this book only involves my actual life experiences and my own opinions. I hope that you will enjoy my story and that you will find answers and explanations to some of the questions that may have been on your mind over time.

Before I begin, let me just say that there can very well be light at the end of the sometimes dark and depressing tunnel. So much depends on how well or how badly you treat your body and how serious you are about dealing with this health condition. Your frame of mind is very important. Either you can allow your condition to put you in a state of depression, or you can face the issue and work with it to your advantage.

Over the past few years, I have always struggled with my sugar levels either going sky-high (hyperglycaemic) or hitting rock bottom (hypoglycaemic). The truth of the matter is, in the beginning, I simply did not take care of myself as I should have. There was always a little devil on my shoulder, waving a chocolate bar, ice cream, or any other delicious sweet treat at me, along with high-carbohydrates foods. **BAM – CFS!!!!!** (Carbs, fats, and sugars!) I simply welcomed these into my body with the thought I'll start again tomorrow. Tomorrow didn't come until many years later. Today, well, I won't say that I don't have some sugar every now and then, but I certainly have cut down a lot on eating it.

A LITTLE BIT ABOUT MY CHILDHOOD

I was born in 1961, in South Africa. I was very fortunate to have had a wonderful childhood. My parents were every child's dream parents when it came to sweets, cakes, and chocolates. I was never denied any of them. I was a very keen eater and didn't struggle with eating meat, fruit, and vegetables, as so many other children seemed to have done at the time. I clearly remember one family in particular wherein the mother used to bribe her children with ice cream or a chocolate treat if they ate the food that was placed on the table in front of them. Fortunately, my mother never had to deal with that problem, and that was probably why I was never denied all the sweet, tasty treats I enjoyed eating so much.

In my early childhood years up to the age of about ten, we didn't have a TV set in our house, so we used to listen to the radio all the time. I distinctly remember one sugar advertisement which used to point out the fact that sugar gives you energy. As any young child is, I was gullible and wanted to have as much energy as possible, so I ate as much sugar as I possibly could. In my mind, I was being good to my body by feeding it all the energy it needed.

When you're a child, your parents are usually your role models, and mine never encouraged me to steer away from the sugar cravings that I had developed in a very big way and at a very early age. I had no idea that I was busy destroying my body by eating so much sugar. As a young child, how was I to know anyway? All I knew was that it tasted good.

Every time my mom went shopping, she would buy me bars of chocolates or anything my little heart desired from the sweets aisle. I loved going shopping with them, because I knew I was going to be spoilt rotten with all those sweet, tasty treats. I'm sure they enjoyed giving them to me and probably thought they were being good, caring, nurturing parents; but the truth of the matter is that they couldn't have realised what they were setting me up to be in my adult years, which would be a diabetic!

My mom would be pushing the shopping trolley up and down the aisles and loading it up with groceries, and I would see something I liked. 'Mommy, can I please have a chocolate?' I would ask. 'Yes, of course, you can,' she would say. I was allowed to choose any chocolate I wanted. At times, I would choose a small one, but most of the time, I would choose a big one. When we walked past the fridges where the ice creams were kept, I would say 'Mommy, please, can we buy some ice cream?' and the ice cream would be put into the trolley. At home, I used to hoard all my sweets and chocolates in one of my desk drawers in my bedroom. It gave me a sense of security, knowing that I would always be able to eat something sweet whenever I felt like it. I wouldn't have to go without them. **BAM** – CFS!!!!!

My dad used to spoil me as well. He was a scuba diver and loved being in the water. He used to go to the local swimming pool on most mornings and would take me with him so I could have a swim while he was exercising. After our swim, he would take me to the local burger joint, which was situated along the beachfront. I always looked forward to having breakfast there. I used to love eating a cheeseburger and fries and drinking a lime-flavoured milkshake, while my dad would order a bacon-and-egg burger and fries.

I used to take my school uniform with me to the swimming pool so that once we had finished eating our breakfast, my dad would take me to school. On the way there, my dad would drive to the local bakery, where he would buy me cream cakes, which I would put into my lunch box for school. **BAM** – CFS!!!!!

I also remember my mom calling out to my dad and I to go and eat dinner at 5 p.m. That is a very early time to have dinner, but that time suited her; she was able to settle down for the night and relax after having a busy day of household chores to catch up on. Unfortunately, by the time it was 7 p.m., I would be hungry again.

My mother used to fry dough which was called vetkoek and give it to my dad and I as a snack. She used to slice it open and fill it with cheese and jam to nibble on. It was meant to keep our appetites satisfied until it was time to go to bed. By then, we had consumed a lot of fat, carbs, and sugar. **BAM** – CFS!!!!!

I do believe that diabetes was probably not as well known then as it is today, because I don't ever remember hearing that disease being mentioned while I was growing up. In my opinion, the diabetic population was probably a lot smaller then than what it is today, because of the fact that home-cooked meals were generally healthier than some of the fast food that we very often eat these days.

WHAT I HAVE LEARNT

As of May 2016:

- There are about 422 million adults worldwide who have diabetes.

- The number of known diabetics has quadrupled since 1980.

- Diabetes kills more people each year than other fatal diseases, such as heart attacks and cancer.

CHAPTER 1

DISCOVERING DIABETES

In 1990, I gave birth to a beautiful baby boy. I was twenty-nine years old at the time. As all mothers know, your whole life changes once you have a little baby to take care of. Everything was fine, but as the months went by, I started getting the most awful migraines. I just put it down to lack of sleep, with having to be up at all hours of the night and all day long too. Then one day, I visited a friend of mine who had three children, all of whom were boys. I told her about the migraines and the continuous thirst I always seemed to have, and she suggested that I let one of her sons, who was a diabetic, prick my finger to check my blood sugar levels. Now needles, blood, and I are as close to one another as the North and South Poles are to each other. I do not like needles, nor do I like blood. So you can imagine how well this 'pricking the finger' thing went. It didn't go well at all! He held my little finger, aimed, and fired. The pain was intense, and there was a stream of blood pouring down my finger. (It was merely a drop, but I need to give you some idea of how much I dislike all this needle and blood stuff.)

The glucometer reading was 14. My friend immediately told me that she thought I was a diabetic and that I needed to make an appointment to see a doctor. To tell you the truth, I had no idea what the meaning of the word diabetes was, so I asked her to explain it to me, which she very briefly did. After her explanation, I must admit I was very suspicious that I might have that terrible disease. The very next day, I made an appointment to see my doctor.

For breakfast, I had a whole can of condensed milk (395 grams)—**BAM** CFS!!!!!—as I very often did. (Just so you know, 100 grams of condensed milk contains 54 grams of sugar.) I had not lost my love of sugary treats. I walked into the doctor's consultation room, sat down, and began explaining my situation to him. I told him that I thought I had a brain tumour. The migraines I was getting were always on the right temple. He smiled and said that before he sent me for a brain scan, he would start by asking me to give him a urine sample and to fast that night and come back the next morning for a blood test. A blood test—no!

When the doctor dipped the strip into the urine sample, he looked at me and asked me what I had eaten prior to seeing him. I told him about the can of condensed milk. He told me he wanted to test my blood for diabetes, along with one or two other things (I don't remember what they were.) So that night, I fasted from midnight onwards, and the next morning, I headed off to Pathology.

I sat down in the chair whilst the pathologist gave me three typed labels to read, check, and sign, making sure that each label had my name and date of birth correctly printed on it. She then took hold of my left arm, told me to stretch it out and form a fist, and inserted the needle into my vein. A vampire was at work! (I'm not referring to her as a vampire; I am referring to the needle and the syringe!) I couldn't bear the thought of her extracting all the blood from my body. I was trying to think of all sorts of different things to take my mind off of what was happening to me. I tried to slow down my heartbeat so that I wouldn't end up dying from a heart attack, and I tried to slow down my sweating rate so that I wouldn't form a pool on the floor and suffer from dehydration. I focused on my teeth, which were attacking my right hand. This was a nightmare in broad daylight, and there was nothing I could do to get away from the situation I was in until it was all over.

I finally heard the sweet, most welcome sound of the pathologist's voice: 'There you go, all done.' She placed a cotton wool bud over the massive hole in my arm and told me to put pressure on it by using my other hand, and that made my stomach turn. I was pushing on a vein in my arm. After she put a sticky strip across the cotton wool to keep it in place, she told me I was free to go, and I walked out of the pathology room feeling very drained and nauseous. I headed straight towards the food court in the mall and ordered a coffee and some breakfast, because even though I was feeling ill, I knew that I needed to get some food into my system.

Every time I talk about having to go to pathology appointments in this story, you can rest assured that they will be no different from this one. Right up until the present day (I am now fifty-seven years old), I still go through the same traumatic experience every time I have a blood test.

I went back to see the doctor three days later so that he could give me the results of the blood tests. I sat down on the opposite side of his table, and he told me my sugar reading level was extremely high. 'Oh, okay,' I said with a smile on my face. I thought that would be obvious. I did, after all, love eating sweet stuff. He then told me I was a diabetic.

'What? Really? Are you sure?' Those were the words that came out of my mouth. The only information I had been given about diabetes was the information my friend had given me. I asked him to explain to me what the disease was all about. After he had told me, he handed me a pamphlet to read, and that was as far as my diabetic education went that day. (In those days, Google was completely unknown. Google was only founded on 4 September 1998, which makes it nineteen years old to date.)

I felt strange when I walked out of his consultation room, knowing I was classified as a diabetic—something I wasn't called just over half an hour ago, before I had gone in to see him. So the time had come for my eating habits to drastically change.

As the weeks and months went by, I found it extremely difficult to do my grocery shopping, attend birthday parties, and go out for lunches and dinners in restaurants; even eating meals at home was hard to do. I wasn't used to the strict, healthy way of eating. Chocolates and ice cream were always my best friends—or so I used to think. Now I was no longer allowed to enjoy eating them, and it didn't stop there. All those delicious fried foods and crispy pork cracklings and absolutely everything else I loved eating so much were suddenly branded with an imaginary Do Not Eat sign.

Oh gosh, my whole world had changed in a flash, and I was as miserable as a grumpy old lady who had been sucking on lemons all day long. How was I going to live through this? I'm sure that if my stomach could have, it would have jumped on to the ground and ran away. The poor thing—it was about to be deprived of so much, not to mention how much my taste buds were going to suffer!

At that point, I was diagnosed as a **Type 2** diabetic, so the medication that was prescribed to me was in tablet form. I had no idea how much my life was about to change later on down the track when I would have to resort to taking insulin injections. It was going to be the toughest time of my life.

Sweet treats are not my best friends.

WHAT I HAVE LEARNT

- In Australia, 280 people develop diabetes every day.

- **Type 1** diabetes accounts for 10% of the diabetic population, and the numbers are rising.

- **Type 2** accounts for 85% of the diabetic population, and the numbers are rising.

CHAPTER 2

THE BEGINNING STAGES OF LIVING MY LIFE AS A DIABETIC

My doctor had put me on a course of tablets. At that stage, as I was a **Type 2** diabetic, that worked well for me. I was absolutely dedicated to eating and drinking the right foods in conjunction with taking the tablets to help control my blood sugar levels. I won't say it was a walk in the park. It started off quite well; but as the first, second, and several more weeks passed by, I started having those dreaded sugar cravings again. I'll tell you what, as history knows it, many wars have been fought and won, but this was a war like no other! Everywhere I went—whether it was while meeting up with friends, grocery shopping, turning on the TV set, or doing anything else—I was faced with the battle of temptation. I would look at a piece of chocolate, and the thought No, that is poison. Do not eat it, would cross my mind. Then suddenly, a little thought would make itself known and say, Oh, for goodness' sake, just eat it. You can always start again tomorrow. And so the war with myself carried on, and eventually, the temptations got the better of me. I started giving in to my sugar cravings by eating a slice of cake here, an ice cream there, and loads of chocolate everywhere. **BAM**-CFS!!!!!

When this was all taking place, my family and I still lived in sunny South Africa. I was married and still am, with two children, a son and a daughter. Let me introduce you to them. My husband's name is Charl. He was born in Zimbabwe, which was originally known as Rhodesia. My son's name is also Charl, and he was born in South Africa. My daughter's name is Carrin, and she was also born in South Africa. My husband, Charl, moved to South Africa, where he studied and got his trade certificate as a diesel mechanic; that was when we met each other and fell hopelessly in love.

Charl always had his heart set on moving back to Zimbabwe one day after he had completed his apprenticeship. He wanted to help his father grow crops on the farm and also work with the cattle, so we eventually decided to move to Zimbabwe. I felt that my husband had lived in my country for a few years, so it was time for me to return the favour and move to his country. Life in South Africa was wonderful, but it was time to experience a new life in Zimbabwe. So in 1998, we made the move.

It was a good one. Life on the farm was great. Charl and his father did exceptionally well with their tobacco sales. At the tobacco sales competitions, they placed in the top five positions for three years running, and in one of those years, they came first and won the trophy.

The only thing that was hard to adjust to was sending our son to boarding school, which was about a one-and-a-half-hour drive away from where we lived in a farming town called Gweru. The good thing was that we used to pick him up from school on Fridays and have him at home with us on the weekends. Because our son has the same name as his father, I will refer to him as CJ in this memoir.

As time went by, I started noticing that I had developed a very big thirst again and, as a result, was always in need of a toilet. I had taken myself off of the prescribed tablets since we had moved to Zimbabwe. I was suspicious that my problem was diabetes related again, so I made an appointment to see another doctor.

The doctor put me back on the same tablets, and life carried on as normal. During that time, I really can't say I was strict about my diet at all. I was very fit in those years. I was younger too. I was completely aware of the implications that were related to incorrect eating and drinking habits in regard to diabetes, but most of us like to think that bad things won't happen to us and that they only happen to others.

Zimbabwe was going through a hard political struggle at the time, and we lived through all of it. I do believe that as a result of that, my body was always functioning on an adrenaline rush, like most people at the time; so I don't think I ever felt the full blow of how ill diabetes could make me feel.

As the years passed, the political situation just got worse, so we decided to apply for immigration to Australia. It took eighteen months before we were given the green light to pack up and leave Zimbabwe, so you can imagine how stressful that was. We were finally accepted into Australia, and in 2002, we landed on Australian soil. Wow, that was a huge step we took; we arrived with no belongings except for the clothes we were wearing and four suitcases of clothing and odds and ends, and Charl brought his tool box full of tools which he would need to use when he started working again.

When we arrived in Australia, we moved into a house in a small country town which is situated in the state of Victoria, and we stayed there for approximately one year before moving on to a farm. It was a beautiful house, and it was situated along the Murray River. We used to go for long walks with the kids and would spend hours fishing from our boat. Life was so relaxing, and over time, we made some wonderful friends who used to come over for visits on the weekends to share the tranquillity of the river with us and who enjoyed being outdoors.

I found a new doctor too who had put me on insulin injections. Now that was an event! I started off using the hospital syringes, so you can only imagine how exciting that would have been for someone who can barely stand the sight of a pin, let alone an injection. I would extract the insulin from the little glass container; flick the syringe to get rid of any air bubbles, like the nurses do in hospitals; bring the needle towards my stomach; grab a roll (one of many); and slowly bring the needle towards the area that was to be pierced. But then it would come to my attention that I needed to go to the toilet. So I would postpone the injection for a few minutes and then start over again with the whole procedure. Ready, aim—oh dear, I would then feel the need to have a cup of coffee, which was much more important to me at that stage than injecting the insulin into my body. After the coffee break, I would pick up the syringe once again, and before I could pierce the needle through my skin, I would then realise that that was the day our dog, Benjamin, had to have his worming tablets. Then I would put the needle down again and attend to Benjamin's needs first.

This used to go on every day. It was a nightmare. Oh my gosh, was there any other way I could get this horrible job done? Eventually, I would manage to get it done, but it would take me at least half an hour to do so; by then I would be so anxious and would have had enough of it. But you have to do what you have to do in life. It took a lot of convincing myself that there was no getting away from this situation and that I would just have to learn how to deal with this phobia I had.

One day we received a phone call from our friends, inviting us to join them on a Sunday afternoon picnic at a lake. It was a beautiful sunny day, so we packed a picnic basket and met them at the lake. We all spent ages swimming and having fun in the sun. When the day was over, we said our goodbyes and headed back home. When we got home, I decided to have a nice cold shower after being in the hot sun all day long. I remember how strange my skin felt as the water trickled down my back. It was a kind of pins-and-needles sensation. It felt so unusual. I had never felt anything like that before whilst having a shower. At the same time, it felt as if my back was literally on fire.

After I had finished having my shower, I asked Charl to rub some cooling gel on my back. That helped a great deal, but the pins-and-needles sensation didn't seem to stop at all. I went to the kitchen and cooked dinner for my family, and then after we had eaten our dinner, we all settled down on the couch to watch a movie on TV.

It must have been about halfway through the show when I started feeling nauseous. I lay there, trying to suppress the nausea, and hoped it would miraculously go away, but to no avail. The next minute, I was in the bathroom, having a long conversation with the big white telephone (in other words, I was throwing up—vomiting).

That was only the beginning. The nausea and vomiting carried on for about a week. I was hoping I was dealing with a stomach bug or a virus that would eventually go away and I would feel better again. Unfortunately, that did not happen; I was getting weaker by the day and losing a lot of weight. Weight loss is a good thing, but it's not good to lose weight in this way. Little did I know that I was going to spend six weeks at a time over the next six years doing exactly the same thing in different hospitals.

WHAT I HAVE LEARNT

- Diabetes mellitus (DM), known as diabetes, is a group of metabolic diseases in which there are high blood sugar levels over a certain period.

- Symptoms to be aware of in cases of high blood sugar levels are an increase of thirst and hunger, along with more urination than usual.

- Acute complications can end in diabetic **ketoacidosis**, non-ketotic hyperosmolar coma, and even death.

- It is important to be treated and to take care of yourself; otherwise, the long-term effects can result in damage to the eyes, kidney failure, heart disease, foot ulcers, and strokes.

CHAPTER 3

BEING ADMITTED INTO THE HOSPITAL FOR THE FIRST TIME

It was April 2003. I couldn't stand the idea of having to go to the hospital, but it was very obvious that I had no choice. My body was so weak I couldn't walk upright anymore. My biggest fear was having to have the IV (intravenous drip) inserted in my arm. As a reminder to you, I am petrified of needles but have had to accept the fact that they will always be a part of my life. It was very much a case of do or die!

After two weeks of my constant nausea and vomiting, the doctors still did their routine rounds every morning and asked me the same questions over and over again. I know this was necessary, but I didn't even have the strength to talk anymore. Having the nurses check my blood sugar readings every hour, being woken up to do ops, and having to listen to the visitors of patients talk about what they were going to make for dinner all added to the discomfort and irritability I was feeling. The thought of the cooked meals on their plates made me throw up even more. I couldn't tolerate the thought of food, and at mealtimes, when the patients' meals were delivered to them, the smell of food turned my stomach inside out.

I told one of the nurses that I wanted to be released from the hospital, which of course, the doctors did not agree with, because it was obvious I was in no condition to be anywhere else at all. When Charl came to visit me one morning, I told him the same thing, and he very reluctantly discussed the matter with one of the doctors. The doctor did not agree with my request to leave the hospital, but I didn't care. So I signed myself out of the ward. I knew I wasn't ready to go home, but the intensity of the noise and not having rest because of all the activity that was going on inside the ward encouraged me to think that if I at least had some peace and quiet at home, it might be to my advantage. I do think though that if I wasn't so ill, the constant activity in the ward would not have been magnified to such a high degree.

When Charl and I arrived at home, I remember the joy I felt, knowing I was with my family again. In the two weeks I had spent in the hospital, I only saw our children twice. The reason for that was that they had school activities to attend to and homework to do. I had lost a lot of weight, so it was probably better that they hadn't seen me looking that way while I was in the hospital. But I was at home with them now, and everything was going to be okay.

I was so proud of CJ and Carrin, because they had done a great job at helping Charl run our home. Our son was a great cook, so he took care of all the meals while I was away; Dad and Carrin kept the house clean and did the laundry.

When we got home, the kids had organised a bed for me, and I was told to lie down or sit up, and relax. My family was wonderful. There wasn't anything that was too much for them to handle, and they pampered me to the max. For a very short while, I felt quite good, but that was only for about half an hour. After that, it was as if the nausea had found me, and it moved right back into my body. We had vomit bags ready to be used, thank goodness, and that's what I did all day and all night long.

All our friends and family knew what was going on, and as can be expected, everyone was very concerned about what this could be leading to. One of our friends suggested I see a naturopath. By then, I was willing to fly to Mars to find someone who could pinpoint the cause and cure of this illness that was chewing me up. Charl took me to see the naturopath, and I remember so clearly how, while we were sitting in the waiting room, I had to lie down on a sofa because I just did not have the strength to sit up anymore. Normally, it would have been embarrassing lying down in the waiting room instead of sitting up, and even more embarrassing throwing up in front of the other patients, but I was so terribly ill that I had no concern for what others thought about me. After what seemed like a very long wait, I was eventually called into the naturopath's consultation room.

He seemed to be very concerned about my condition, and he was enthusiastic about the fact that we could get to the bottom of this problem. I had a lot of faith in him, and although I couldn't even have a full consultation without having to throw up and felt as if death was just moments away, he managed to drag a little bit of hope out of my soul that there would be light at the end of the tunnel. He meant well, and Charl and I left his room with two containers of tablets, a bottle of syrup, and a selection of energy bars.

Once we got back home, I was on a mission to conquer whatever was going on inside my body, and Charl brought me a glass of water so that I could start taking the tablets. Immediately after swallowing the first one, I vomited. The same applied when I tried to swallow the syrup about an hour later, and as far as eating an energy bar was concerned, well, that didn't work either. That was the situation I had been in for a few weeks already, and although I tried to convince myself I would be quite fine with being out of the hospital, it was very obvious once again that that was the only place where I should be, because at least if I was there, I would be put on the drip again and would remain hydrated.

It turned out my hope of being at home for a long time did not materialise, because on the very next day, Charl took me back to the hospital. It was the same story all over again—an absolute nightmare! The nausea and vomiting into vomit bags, feeling irritated when the doctors and nurses worked on me, and once again, the sound of voices and the smell of food that was brought to the other patients were all repetitions of what I had to put up with as I lay in the hospital bed, feeling like death warmed up, as the saying goes.

It's amazing how you just can't tolerate anything or anyone around you when your world is turned upside down. You want everyone to respect the fact that you are not well, but through your eyes, nobody seems to care. The truth of the matter is that life goes on. Other people's lives go on, and nobody can be expected to stop doing what they are doing because you are not well. But at the time it is all happening, you think of everyone as being quite inconsiderate. In their worlds, they haven't got a clue what you are thinking or exactly how you are feeling. I'd look out of the hospital window and see birds flying in the sky and would even envy them! It was a very strange feeling.

I used to look at everyone and wish I could leave my body and pop into theirs. The one thing that really frustrated me was the fact that the patients' visitors would bring their children with them to the hospital and allow the children to run around the ward and make a noise. Hospitals are places where sick people go to, for goodness' sake. They are not children's playgrounds! Some of the parents were no better. They used to talk and laugh so loudly. It sounded like they were attending a comedy show. It was terrible lying in bed in that condition when there were so many inconsiderate, rowdy people.

When I thought things could not get any worse, I woke up one morning to a lot of banging and drilling going on right outside the ward window and soon discovered that renovations were taking place on the hospital building.

Tears streamed down my face. Did those builders not care how ill I was feeling? Of course not! Why would they care? I do realise that they had a job to do, but when you are feeling as desperately ill as I was, your emotions tend to get the better of you.

The nurses were a nice crowd of ladies. They were always cheerful and were always trying to make the patients feel light-hearted. It didn't work for me though. The only thing that would have made me happy would have been to know what was going on inside my body. I told Charl that I didn't think I would ever live a normal life again, and I firmly believed that. I was convinced that the situation I was in was infinite.

One day, a lovely old lady walked into the ward and headed straight towards me. She took my hand and told me that she had heard things were not going too well with me, that I need not worry because God was looking after both my family and me, and that I would be healed in His time. He wanted me to be patient. Time! I thought. How much more time does God need to heal me? He performs miracles, doesn't He? The word patience no longer existed in my vocabulary. I wanted to be healed there and then! She told me everything was going to be all right. I wanted to fast-forward the journey and live in the part where everything was indeed all right!

By then, with all the vomiting that had been going on, I had lost the use of my vocal chords. The only way I could communicate was by whispering, and even that was an effort. Anyway, I managed to whisper to her that I wanted to get out of the hospital—again! This darling, dear old lady offered to take me to her house, where she said the atmosphere was very tranquil.

Charl arrived at the hospital about half an hour after she did, and he also got to meet her. She told him how she had been talking to me and encouraging me by saying God would heal me. She also told Charl God would give him the strength he needed to keep going while this illness was attacking me. It felt good to have her there, because both Charl and I are firm believers in God. We are of the Christian faith.

She told him she would be very happy to take me home to her house, which wasn't far from the hospital at all and where she felt a lot of healing would take place; I would be able to relax and get enough rest without the hustle and bustle of the hospital. I was very upset and desperate for a miracle to happen, because it felt like lying in the hospital and continuously having my blood pressure, sugar readings, medications, etc. done just wasn't getting me anywhere. I felt trapped in a time zone where there was no way out. Every day was as bad as the previous one. I felt as if I wasn't moving forward or getting any better.

My husband finally agreed to it, because we lived a fair distance out of town; I would at least have someone looking after me all day and night. If I went home, he would have had to take time off work, and if he wasn't given time off, I would be alone at home, which wouldn't have been a good thing. So thankfully, I once again signed myself out of the hospital, and Charl took me to the lady's house. It was a bit weird accepting a stranger's invitation to stay at her house, but I was so desperate to be in a quieter environment.

The poor lady must have felt so helpless with trying to make me feel comfortable all the time. Gospel music was always playing in the background. She believed it would be very soothing, but the truth of the matter was that I wanted her to turn it off. She had a little dog, such a darling little thing; he always used to come up to me whilst I lay on the couch, and he wanted me to pat him. I love dogs, but even something as affectionate and cute as that irritated me to no end. When you are nauseous and constantly vomiting, I don't think winning the lottery would even have mattered, because without your health, you have nothing!

The lovely old lady was constantly offering me food and drinks. She was always taking such good care of my needs, but they were all things

I didn't need or want. After three days of being in this loving, caring environment, I sent my husband a text message, asking him to please pick me up and take me home.

He arrived at the house that afternoon and told me that if I ended up in the hospital one more time (which was very obviously going to happen), he would insist I stay there until the doctors had discovered what was going on with me and cured the problem. I thanked the lady, and we headed home one more time. There was something about going for a drive in the car. I noticed that that was the only time the vomiting would settle down. The nausea was always there, but I would stop vomiting as long as I was lying down on the back seat of the car, face down, on my stomach.

The next few days were very hard indeed. I actually couldn't remember the last time any day was an easy one. Charl had to be at work, and the kids had to attend school; so this time I was alone at home. In a way, it was probably a very good thing, because it gave me time to realise that I couldn't possibly function on my own. There was nothing I could do for myself, because I was so terribly weak! My muscles hadn't worked properly in about six weeks, and I had lost so much weight. To tell you the truth, I had lost 10 kilograms (22 pounds) over a period of six weeks. On the day that I first went into the hospital, I weighed 55 kilograms (121 pounds), and after six weeks, I weighed 45 kilograms (96 pounds). With me being of small build, 1.52 metres (5 feet), I looked like a skeleton. I'll tell you what, I have never lost so much weight with dieting in my life.

My darling husband, who was sick with worry about me, phoned me from work during the day to hear how I was doing. The answer was always the same—weak with nausea and vomiting. At about lunchtime, I tried to perform this 'mind over matter' thing. I dragged myself out of bed, and whilst holding on to the walls, I made my way into the dining room at a snail's pace and opened the sliding french doors that led into the back garden. There were two steps that led from the dining room into the garden, and it was an absolute mission trying to walk down those two steps. My body was seizing up, and I had to do something about it. I had to somehow get exercise to kick-start my muscles again. I would say that the only thing that made me carry on with trying to get out of the house was sheer determination. Once I had accomplished that very difficult task, which carried on for about five minutes, I started making my way to the front gate so that I could go for a 'walk' along the pathway.

It was very hard. I didn't have the strength to hold my body up straight, and I hardly had the strength to put one foot in front of the other. But I had to keep on trying. Of course, with each step I took came the feeling of nausea. After walking for about 20 metres (65 feet), I realised I had to start making my way back to the house again. I left the house at approximately twelve noon, and by the time I got back home, it was already one p.m. It took me a full hour to walk just over 40 metres (130 feet) in total. I seriously doubt I would have won a gold medal at the Olympics.

It was a great feeling when my husband and children came home from work and school. I felt so comfortable having them there with me. As soon as they got home, they started cooking dinner and made me comfortable on the couch so that we could all be in the lounge together, watching TV during the night. That was fantastic, but the only problem I was faced with was the fact that I was still throwing up into vomit bags.

Now let me just say something. During this time, I had seen, in total, six doctors, and they were all still wondering what the cause of my condition was. They knew I was a diabetic, but they could not seem to get to the core of the problem. After visiting all of them and finding no resolution to the problem, I started to feel as if they could not deal with me anymore. Although they tried everything they could to help me, I was a mysterious case, and so I started to feel as if I was going to end up dying. Then one of Charl's work colleagues told him about a certain

Doctor Drake, whom he believed might be able to get to the root of the problem, so Charl made an appointment to see him.

When we walked into his room, he looked like a very stern type of man. That didn't worry me at all. I was just in need of someone who could save my life. We sat down, and Charl did all the talking, because I didn't have the energy to hold a conversation. Charl took the doctor on the long, hard journey we were on and told him how desperately in need we were of finding a cure. The doctor was very keen and determined to find out what was going on. After listening to Charl talk, he said it sounded as if I was suffering from neuropathic complications. I was absolutely thrilled that he had come up with something new to try out, and he said that he would contact the hospital and have a chat with them but that I would have to be readmitted on the same day. This time, I was to stay there until I was completely healed.

Right after the doctor's appointment, Charl took me back to the hospital once again, and this time they insisted that I wasn't allowed to sign myself out and that I would have to stay there until I was officially released by one of the doctors.

I have to say that by that time, I felt extremely frustrated with having been in and out of the hospital for two months already, and there had still been no improvement at all with my medical condition. As I lay in the hospital bed, with nurses constantly checking my blood pressure, temperature, and sugar readings, I felt like a cork that was continuously bobbing up and down, not reaching any destination, not reaching any goals. I had become very sensitive to everything that was going on all around me. When the nurses pricked my finger to test my blood sugar readings, it felt as if they squeezed so hard before piercing my skin with the needle. I kept on thinking, Stop doing things to me that aren't making any difference! They were doing what needed to be done, but I was over all of it by that time.

In the meantime, while all this was going on, Charl decided to start doing some research of his own to hopefully get to the bottom of this medical condition that I had had for ages. All I can say is, thank goodness for the Internet, which he was then able to make use of.

He did a lot of work with typing in all the symptoms that were related to my condition. He read each and every one of them and printed them out. My darling husband was absolutely exhausted, carrying the burden of worry for such a long time. As a result of his research, Charl also came to the conclusion that I had a neuropathic problem. He made another appointment to see the doctor, and when he went into the consultation room, he took out his researched notes and placed them on the doctor's table for him to read. The doctor was very impressed with Charl's research indeed. It sounded as if my husband had got hold of the answer we had been looking for. It appeared that the diabetes could possibly have damaged nerves in my stomach.

Doctor Drake communicated with the doctors at the hospital, and I was booked for a gastroscopy, where the results came back negative. So there we were—back to square one. We still had no idea what was going on.

The feeling of absolute helplessness overwhelmed me once again. It overwhelmed my entire family, to be honest. Was I meant to die like this? How much longer would this have to go on for? I had made the decision to finally give up on life. I lay in the hospital bed and thought about my family and the friends who I would be leaving behind, but after being so ill for such a long time, I really didn't care anymore. I asked Charl to bring the children to the hospital so that I could see them, but he refused to do so. He said that if I wanted to see them again, I would have to survive this ordeal. Oh my gosh, I couldn't take it anymore. I was worried that if I did pass away, he would have to live with a guilty conscience for the rest of his life because he had denied me the privilege of seeing them one more time. What a brave act to carry out. That was how far he was willing to go to give me a reason to want to live. Charl is my hero!

As the week passed, I was still being fed medications through the drip. It felt like the vomiting and nausea was there to stay! The nightmare carried on, but somehow the nausea eventually started easing off, slowly but surely. The nurses carried on with their routines and brought me tablets for the pain and nausea (because I did still have to deal with that). I was given tablets for bowel movement. Because I wasn't able to stomach food, my bowel hadn't worked in weeks. I was taking so many tablets and decided not to take them anymore. Every time the nurses gave me tablets, I pretended to swallow them. When they left my bedside, I'd open up my handbag and put the tablets in it. Do you want to know how I felt once I started doing that? Oh my gosh, I started feeling so much better!

On one of Charl's visits, I told him I wasn't taking the medication that was being given to me. I told him that I was so exhausted and that I was starting to feel like I was a living pharmacy. I was swallowing tablets and being injected with medications, but it seemed like they were not doing anything for me. I didn't feel any different; I just remained in the same old sick mode I was in two and a half months before. I can fully understand how he was concerned to hear that. A little bird told me he might have whispered my secret into someone's ear, because after that, the nurses would not leave my bedside until they had seen me drink from the cup and swallow the tablets. But I kept the tablets securely tucked away on the inner side of my mouth and gulped the water down, making it look as if I had done what was expected of me. You must realise that when you have been that ill and have almost come face-to-face with death on numerous occasions, you start taking the initiative, and you start listening to your mind and body. This might sound crazy, but it is a fact!

In spite of the fact that I had started feeling better, the nausea and vomiting seemed to have moved right back into my body once again. The smell of breakfasts, lunches, and dinners being served to the other patients; the sound of people's voices; the nurses taking my hand, pricking my finger and drawing blood, strapping the blood pressure monitor to my arm, and putting the thermometer in my ear; the sound of the cleaner changing the bin bags; and absolutely everything else made me feel nauseous. It was as if I had developed an intolerance to anything and everything.

As the days went by, I started getting extremely anxious and frustrated that we were not getting to the bottom of the problem. I knew my darling husband and Dr. Drake were desperately looking for an answer to what was going on, but to be trapped inside a shell with no way of getting out made me feel very claustrophobic. I had been praying to God, asking Him to please get me out of the situation I was so tired of being in for such a long time. But I then went one step further and turned my prayer request around and started asking Him to take my life! I told Him that if He wanted me, I was ready to leave this life and move on to the next one. Once I had reached the point where I was in that frame of mind, I had literally given up on life. I no longer had the desire to get better. Before that happened though, I had given so much thought to wanting to get well again and spend the rest of my life with my beautiful husband and two children, and of course, our dear friends.

My prayer resources were exhausted, and my level of caring had gone down to less than zero. From worrying about how my husband would cope without me and wanting to be alive to see our children grow up, have successful lives, and get married one day, which would allow us to experience a wonderful life with our grandchildren, I had reached a point where I told myself my husband would eventually be fine after I passed away. He would probably meet and marry someone else and be happy, and my children would come to terms with my passing and would carry on, living their lives as normal. At the end of the day, none of us can escape death. In fact, it's probably the only thing we can be 100 per cent sure of. After all these thoughts had gone through my mind over what seemed like a thousand times, I was finally ready to let go and move on to the next life, be it heaven or hell—but very hopefully, it was going to be heaven.

In the meantime, one of the doctors had told Charl that he simply did not know what else to do for me. My health situation was a complete mystery, and they were not having any joy with solving the problem. It felt as if they had gone down every avenue to make me well again but couldn't find the solution to the problem; therefore, to me, it felt as if I was heading towards the end of the road.

I whispered to Charl to please bring the kids to see me, because as can be expected, I wanted to say a few things to them before I died. But my very brave husband refused me the right to see them once again, unless I got better! Better? It was very obvious that was not going to happen—ever! I was worried to death (pun), to say the least, at the thought of never seeing or talking to my children again. I needed to give them some untold advice about life as they were growing up, and I needed to tell them that I knew they would miss me like crazy and be sad to no end. I needed to tell them that I would rather have got through all this turmoil and spent the rest of my life enjoying seeing them grow up; I needed to tell them that their dad and the doctors had pretty much done all they could to save me, but the time had come for me to move on to the next life. I needed to tell them that death is the one thing you have to accept, whether you want to or not.

All I can say is that my husband is one hell of a man! I mean, can you imagine how much guilt he would have had to suffer if I had passed away? He meant well, but it wouldn't have worked out too well for him if it had truly been my time to go.

When I hit rock bottom, Charl had a chat with one of the doctors, who agreed to have me moved to a private ward in order to give me some rest from all the activity that was going on in the general ward. I was taken up to the maternity ward, which was completely different from the general ward I had been in for so long. It was colourful and was something you would see in everyday living, but it had become a luxury to me. There was a painting on one of the walls, and there were curtains hanging from the pelmet. It looked like a scene from a movie. It was just beautiful, and there was a distinct calmness about the atmosphere. I also found the nurses to be soft-spoken, and they had the traditional ways of being respectful towards patients. The room also had its own bathroom. I felt a slight nudge of life flowing through my body and soul, and I was quite happy to spend the rest of my hospital days there.

The next morning, after I had been moved to the maternity ward, I woke up and went to the bathroom (as we all do), and while I was in there, Charl arrived to visit me. Not long after that, I heard another familiar voice in the ward. I wasn't too sure if it could have possibly been my ex–best friend, Chez. At some stage, Chez and I had a disagreement that took us to a bad place with one another, and we hadn't seen each other in approximately three months. I used to—and still do—adore that woman. We were the perfect match, as far as friends were concerned. Now I was 10 kilograms (22 pounds) lighter and very weak, and my posture was in the shape of a bent-over great-grandmother!

I opened the bathroom door, and there she stood! Was I dreaming or imagining what was happening in front of me? Then in her usual casual, honest way—just the way I like her to be—she said, 'Hello, my friend. What the hell is wrong with you? You look like shit! Why are you taking such a long holiday, just lying around the place and doing nothing?' and walked up to me and gave me a huge hug. Well, as can be expected, the tears streamed down both our faces. I swear, if we had our swimming costumes with us, we could have dived into a pool of water!

Charl helped me get back on to the bed, and the three of us had the time of our lives! For the first time in what seemed like a century, I actually found a reason to giggle, because of some of the things she said. You know the expression 'Talk about having a breath of fresh air'? Well, that was the real deal! For the next fifteen minutes or so (that was all the time she could spare with me because of her work commitments), I didn't feel any nausea, only pure joy and excitement. I had forgotten what that even felt like over the past few weeks. It felt amazing, and the person whom I owed all that gratification to was my darling husband.

He had gone the extra mile and was so desperate for me to have some interest in life that he contacted Chez and told her what had been going on over the past few months and asked her to visit me in the hospital.

It was so easy for us to carry on where we had left off from all those months ago. That is what I call a genuine friendship. You don't find too many of those kinds of friends in this world these days. Her visit was short and very sweet, but she told me she was going to come back that night for a long decent visit, which she did. She brought with her a pair of new pajamas that she had bought for me. It felt so nice to receive a gift from her.

That night, when Chez came for a visit, she had me in stitches. I told her she was a miracle. I can't emphasise enough how much better I was feeling. When the nurse came to do my ops, she said it was common knowledge amongst the nursing staff that I hadn't smiled once since the first time I was admitted into the hospital. I wonder why? LOL! Oh wow, now that I've used the word LOL, it just reminded me I haven't had a look at my Facebook page today. LOL! Anyway, let's get back to my story.

I think once Chez came into the picture, it was a kind of relief for Charl. He was so happy to see his wife's face glowing for a change and was so pleased to hear some positivity in her voice. In a nutshell, this was the beginning of my recovery period. I suddenly found the will to live again. The only way I can explain myself is to say that Chez's funny sense of humour triggered a spark in my system, and when I saw how happy Charl was to see me smile, that spark turned into a towering inferno! My darling husband had been feeling terrible for such a long time, watching me in this condition day after day. When I saw the joy in his face, it was so uplifting, and it gave me the will to fight for my life again. He had had enough of feeling anxious and desperate, as much as I had had enough of being violently ill.

I spent the next four days in the maternity ward, and it was like putting my finger in the wall socket and having my batteries charged. On the morning of the fifth day, one of the nurses came to me and told me they needed my bed for a pregnant lady who was on her way to the hospital to give birth to her baby. It felt like the walls were tumbling down all around me. I couldn't bear the thought of being taken back to the general ward, but I had no choice.

So once again, I was amongst all the noise of the other patients' visitors and the hysteria of naughty screaming children who seemed to be under the impression that the hospital ward was a racetrack. Grr, I must have grinded a lot of my teeth away (pun). In fact, sometimes I would get so annoyed I wished I could yell out to everyone to shut their mouths. I mean, let's face it, when you are ill, the last thing you need around you is a bunch of noisy voices.

Charl couldn't emphasise enough to the doctors how important it was to get my bowels to start moving. With all the experience we had had with me being so ill, he also noticed that whenever my bowels weren't working, I would start feeling unwell. Eventually, the nausea and vomiting lessened, and over a period, it completely disappeared. I was getting visits from my friends and family, which was great because I could smile again and engage in conversations, unlike before. The highlight of my hospital stay was when one of the nurses disconnected the drip from my arm, and I was a free woman again! I started eating the meals that were offered to me, and now that I could stomach the smell and taste of food, it was an absolute luxury to eat and enjoy the hospital chef's cooking. With food going into my stomach and with the help of the bowel medication, I finally got the urge to go to the toilet! It was such a celebration I told everyone who came to visit me that day that I had pooped! Wow, I never thought so much joy could ever come about from talking about my poop, but it sure did.

There was yet another highlighted moment which was also much-needed. One of the doctors paid me a visit early in the morning and asked me a few questions, and of course, one of them was 'Has your bowel moved yet?' With great pride, I answered, 'Yes, Doctor.' He nodded and told me that was good, and then he proceeded to say that I could be released from the hospital by late afternoon the following day. I'll tell you what, at that moment, even the ward, with all its goings-on, looked so different through my eyes. I was, metaphorically speaking, in heaven!

Charl arrived at the hospital in the morning to be given the good news, and after lunchtime, he arrived again and waited with me until the nurse brought the release form for me to sign. How exciting! I was going to experience the feeling of the warm sun on my skin again, and I was going to be involved in everyday living. I could not wait to be a part of that. It goes without saying, though, that it did take a lot of time and effort for me to get my muscles up and going to their full capacity again. When Charl and I went to town to do our shopping, for example, I walked at a snail's pace. It took a good three to four weeks before I was fully mobile again, but I enjoyed every minute of the day and have never again taken for granted waking up in the morning, stepping out of bed, and walking into the kitchen to turn the kettle on.

WHAT I HAVE LEARNT

The Difference between Type 1 and Type 2 Diabetes

TYPE 1

Beta cells in the pancreas are attacked by the body's own immune system, which results in the reduction of producing insulin, which in turn leads to high blood glucose levels. Insulin is only produced in small amounts or is not produced at all.

TYPE 2

The consumption of too much dietary sugar leads to great demands on insulin production, and over a long period, this results in insulin resistance. Receptor cells that have resistance to insulin are not able to remove glucose from the blood; therefore, this leads to higher blood glucose and greater demands on insulin production.

CHAPTER 4

MOVING TO A WARMER PART OF THE COUNTRY

It was really nice to be able to enjoy the next few months at home with my family, and feeling healthy and happy was great. During that time, our lives had got back to normal, and it was also great being involved with our friends again.

It was the beginning of winter, and I started getting very bad pains in my legs and feet. So Charl made another appointment for me to see Doctor Drake, who suggested we move to a warmer part of the country. We were under the impression that, with what was being said, the insulin was thickening my blood, which was causing the pain in my legs, because of the cold weather.

Our friends, Chez and Richard, were also planning to move to a different part of the country and had decided to do a road trip to the state of Queensland. Because that was our plan too, we arranged with them that I would go on the trip as well so that I could also put my feelers out as to where I thought Charl and I might want to move. It was a great trip, and after having travelled 3,000 kilometres (1,864 miles), we were happy to be back at home again. After having a chat with Charl, we decided to move to Queensland. Within one month of having made that decision, we sold a lot of our household items, packed up the rest, and headed for warmer climate.

After living in a caravan park for at least three weeks, we finally found a house to rent and settled down quite quickly.

Life got very busy, with Charl having to go to work, the kids attending school, and me running the home. Within a few months' time, I decided to start looking for a job to help pay the bills. I found an office job at one of the freight companies that paid a nice enough salary, and we were doing very well for ourselves. We also found a new family doctor. My three monthly BSL (blood sugar level) readings were in the 7s and even went up to 8. I was getting my normal prescriptions for insulin injections and happily lived through each and every day.

Then one day, whilst I was at my desk at work, I suddenly felt a sick feeling in my stomach. Because I had lived with that feeling for such a long time in the past, I immediately knew what to expect. That was how I was feeling the first time I ended up in the hospital and every other time after that. I urgently needed to get to the toilet, and I was so relieved to find it wasn't occupied. There was only one ladies' toilet within the company. Well, blow me over—there it was again. It was that awful fruity flavour in my mouth and the dark, almost-black colour coming up and out of my throat when I vomited. The illness had tracked me down from my previous home in Victoria to my present home here in Queensland.

Once I felt I could go back to my desk, I ended up running to the toilet twice again after that. I phoned my husband, who, fortunately for me, was at home at the time, and he told me he was on his way to pick me up from work. As soon as I got into Charl's car, the first thing he said to me was that he could smell that fruity odour in my breath. Oh, dear Lord, was this really happening again? When we got home, I packed my bags without hesitation, and we headed for the hospital!

The whole experience of being in the hospital again was a repetition of what had previously happened, and once again, I was attached to the dreaded drip.

Dehydration is a killer. When you are constantly vomiting throughout the day and night, you are sure to suffer from dehydration, as we all know, and the only way to stay hydrated is by going to the hospital and relying on the drip.

As the days passed, I went into a state of depression. Because I was so ill, it felt as if I had dealt with so much discomfort yet was still left with no answers. I was sent to have an ultrasound and a CT scan. It was eventually determined that my gall bladder was the cause of my illness, so it had to be removed. It was actually a very exciting event. I thought we had got to the root of all this evil, but that was merely a figment of my imagination. I was picturing myself never having to go to the hospital again once the gall bladder had been removed. An appointment was made for me to have keyhole surgery.

Once that was all over, I felt a lot better, and eventually I felt as normal as the next person. I was very relieved I didn't have to spend weeks in the hospital again and could carry on with normal day-to-day living.

WHAT I HAVE LEARNT

Diabetes Affects Nerve Endings

Having high blood glucose for many years can damage the blood vessels that bring oxygen to some nerves, as well as the nerve coverings. Damaged nerves may stop sending messages or may send messages too slowly or at the wrong times. Numbness, pain, and weakness in the hands, arms, feet, and legs may develop. Problems may also occur in various organs, including the digestive tract, heart, and sex organs. Diabetic neuropathy is the medical term for damage to the nervous system from diabetes. The most common type is peripheral neuropathy, which affects the arms and legs.

The highest rates of neuropathy are amongst people who have had the disease for at least twenty-five years and, in those with high levels of blood fat and blood pressure, in overweight people over the age of forty.

You can help keep your nervous system healthy by keeping your blood glucose as close to normal as possible, getting regular physical activity, not smoking, taking good care of your feet each day, having your healthcare provider examine your feet at least four times a year, and getting your feet tested for nerve damage at least once a year.

CHAPTER 5

MY FIRST TRIP TO AND FROM SOUTH AFRICA

It was May 2013, and my mother was about to celebrate her seventieth birthday. She lived in Cape Town, South Africa, and I desperately wanted to visit her for that very special occasion. I flew from Brisbane, Australia, to Malaysia, and then finally to South Africa to visit her. It was wonderful seeing my mom and my two sisters, Pat and Allison. They were waiting for me at the international arrivals area at the airport. I hadn't seen any of them in about twenty-six years. It's amazing how much people change with age over the years. My oldest sister, Allison, called out to me, and it was ever so exciting seeing those three wonderful ladies again after such a long time. We never lived in the same house, with my dad having been married to their mother before he met and married mine. The greetings at the airport were quite emotional. My mom told me she had seen me coming through customs and thought I looked a bit like her daughter, which made me realise that I must have changed quite a bit too over the years.

After we were finished with all the hugs and kisses, we climbed into Allison's car and drove to her house, where she had prepared a delicious lunch which consisted of cold meats and salads. Well, guess what? Don't let me keep you guessing for too long. Yes, you guessed right—I started feeling nauseous, and it didn't take long before I was bending over the toilet again and retching my heart out. I knew straight away that this was not going to end well. With it being the month of May, I would like to say that old habits die hard, because my normal 'check-in time' in hospitals was always either April or May; the fact remained that the same tradition still carried on. Nothing had really changed, in spite of the fact that my gall bladder had been removed.

My sister Allison gave me tablets to take the nausea away, but that did not help at all. After a very miserable two hours or so, Allison took my mother and me to my mother's apartment, and I settled down and went straight to bed. Unfortunately, that didn't take away any of the symptoms. The next day, Allison phoned my mom to find out how I was feeling. After telling her there was no improvement at all in my condition, Allison phoned my mother's doctor and made an appointment for me to see him that same day. A few hours later, my sister arrived at my mom's apartment to pick us up, and we headed off to see the doctor.

I was obviously very familiar with what was happening to me, but I was still unaware of what the cause of the problem was. I hoped that doctor would be the person whom I had been waiting for, for such a long time, and who would be able to pinpoint the reason for this illness.

We were called into the doctor's consultation room. After all the questions he asked me and after me giving him a full explanation about what had happened to me in the past, his analysis on what was causing me to feel so terribly ill was that I had probably picked up a stomach bug from somewhere. A stomach bug! And not just a stomach bug, but one I seemed to pick up at the same time every year. He sent me on my way with some tablets and told me to rest. I knew there and then that this holiday was going to be no holiday at all. I was also very concerned that it might turn out to be yet another six weeks in the hospital in South Africa, of which two of the six weeks would be spent in ICU. I spent the first five days of the first week I was in South Africa lying on the couch in the lounge. It was terrible, and all I kept on thinking about was the fact that I did not want to end up going to the hospital again, because once I was there, I might not be able to come out in time to go home again.

Strangely enough, I started feeling slightly better after five days, and Allison thought it would be a good idea to get me out of the apartment for the day. She contacted her son, Sean (my nephew), and asked him if he would take us for a nice long drive to do some sightseeing and stop over at a restaurant for lunch. He was more than happy to do that for us, and he and Allison picked my mom and me up.

When I got into the car, I felt squeamish. My stomach was letting me know that the drive was not going to be at all pleasant, but I guess I wanted to suppress the feeling and hoped it would go away, even if it was just for that one day.

As we travelled along the road, I admired the view. It was stunning. Cape Town was a beautiful city. We were driving on the outskirts, and I remember how beautiful and green the fields were. It was such a picturesque scene. We had been travelling in the car for approximately two hours, when I suddenly had the urge to throw up. I whispered to my mom that I needed to throw up, and she asked Sean to please pull over as soon as possible. He was unable to stop the car, because there was a string of cars behind us. I had no choice but to roll the window down, hang my head out, and vomit. It was much better than getting sick inside the car, but unfortunately, it all went down the side of the car door.

Sean was eventually able to pull over to the side of the road, and I climbed out of the car and knelt on the ground. It was awful. I vomited repeatedly, and I could hear someone saying, 'Don't worry, you'll be fine.' At the time, I had no idea whose voice I had heard, and the person was stroking my hair whilst this was all going on. I just remember wanting that very kind person to stop doing that. I wanted to be left alone. I wasn't feeling very elegant, being bent over and spreading my body fluids all over the ground. The vomiting eventually eased off, and I was able to get back into the car. The nausea was still there though. Allison told Sean to take me to a pharmacy which was about a twenty-minute drive away to try and get some form of medication that would make me feel better.

We eventually arrived at the pharmacy. It took me ages to get out of the car, because by that time, the cramps in my stomach were quite severe. The pharmacist asked me one or two questions, but I was unable to speak. Allison did all the talking for me. He gave her some tablets to give to me to stop the nausea, but I shook my head. I knew I was not going to be able to stomach them. She opened up the container and told me to try and swallow one. The pharmacist handed me a glass of water, and there I was—the star of the show! Everyone was waiting and wondering if I was going to be able to swallow and stomach the tablets. I knew it was going to be impossible to do, but I had an audience; every single one of them wanted me to get the meds in so that I could start feeling better. I put the first tablet in my mouth, took a swig of water, swallowed, and vomited it up. The pharmacist told me to try again. I know he meant well, but I felt a burst of frustration come over me. Could the man not see that swallowing and keeping the tablet down was an impossible mission I simply could not carry out!

He told Allison and Sean they should get me to the nearest hospital as soon as possible. Allison told Sean that we had no option but to turn the car around and head back home, which is what we did. Unfortunately for everyone, we never got to have that lovely lunch in the fancy restaurant we were all looking forward to visiting. Poor Allison, Sean, and my mom were quite hungry by then, so we pulled up at a little takeaway place so that everyone could buy themselves something to eat. I remember how considerate Allison was when she told Sean and my mom not to buy any greasy food, because the smell would make me throw up again. Poor Sean was less than impressed, I think, when he noticed the vomit streaks on the side of his new car.

Anyway, everyone bought food and drinks, and we were on the road once again, homeward-bound.

Once we reached my mother's apartment, Allison phoned her doctor, and we were given an appointment time immediately. He also asked me several questions, but Allison was still my voice. He too came to the conclusion that I must have picked up a virus of some sort. I was given a prescription and was sent home once again to rest.

By then, I was mentally and physically exhausted, and all I could think about was the fact that we were fighting a losing battle with this mysterious condition. I just wanted this horrible thing, whatever it was, to go away, and I also wanted to be at home with my husband and my children. My concern was that I might not be able to get home to them by the due date, because if I did end up in the hospital, it might turn out to be another six-week stay.

All I wanted was to feel healthy again. I wanted to feel what it was like to wake up in the morning and not have nausea and vomiting. I found myself being envious of every living being around me. How fortunate are we to have health on our side? This is something the average person takes for granted.

My family in South Africa tried to encourage me not to fly home whilst I was in that condition, but all I wanted to do was get home, regardless of how I was feeling at the time. I knew this illness was going to be attached lock, stock, and barrel to my body, and I didn't want to be away from home for an extra six weeks, because that always seemed to be the period that I would end up being in the hospital. (I was glad that I did go to South Africa then, because that was going to be the last time I would ever see my dad alive. He passed away only a few weeks after I had returned to Australia.)

The day had finally arrived for me to fly back home to Australia. Allison told me that if I wasn't feeling well, she would not take me to the airport. I felt awful but managed to put on a very brave act. There was nothing that was going to stop me from boarding that aircraft! The plan that morning was to have a farewell breakfast at the airport with Pat, Allison, and my mom. Everyone was feeling emotional, which is normal when family and friends have to say goodbye to one another, but the only person who wasn't feeling that way was me. Not because I didn't have a soft heart, but because while everyone was sitting around the breakfast table, I was in the ladies' room, having a chat with that big white telephone once again! While I was bent over the toilet, it was announced that all passengers who were on my flight were to board the aircraft. I literally dragged myself to the airport restaurant, where we all said our goodbyes. I was literally too ill to feel sad, and once again, Allison asked me if I felt well enough to board the plane. I had to board that plane, no matter what!

Once I was sitting in my seat in the aircraft, I felt a huge relief. I was finally on my way home. The plane took off, and all I can say is, thank goodness I only threw up twice on that flight, which was a complete surprise to me. The nausea was constant, but I kept on telling myself to hang in there. I was heading home to get well. How, I did not know, but there had to be light at the end of this very dark tunnel! When I felt like throwing up, it was fortunate for both myself and the other passengers that I managed to make it to the toilet in time and that there was always one vacant.

After being airborne for approximately nine hours, we landed in Kuala Lumpur, Malaysia. The aircraft doors were finally opened, and the passengers started moving to the front of the plane to exit it. I remained in my seat and waited until every single passenger had disembarked. I then stood up and made my way to the exit too. Before I left the aircraft, I asked one of the air hostesses if I could have a bottle of water to take into the airport terminal with me. I felt extremely dehydrated, and fortunately, without hesitation, she handed me a bottle of water, which I immediately opened and gulped down. What I am about to tell you next might sound quite unbelievable.

As I made my way into the airport terminal, I felt like death warmed up (not quite like a zombie, but very close to that). I then went to the information desk to ask for directions to the minibus that I knew I was supposed to be on, which would take me to the hotel I was booked into for the day. I was supposed to rest and freshen up before having to fly out again at 2 a.m. the following day to Brisbane, Australia. Before arriving at the hotel, the nausea got so bad again, and all I remember saying was 'I want to get sick!' One of the other passengers in the minibus, an Asian lady, told the driver to pull over. He did that, and there I was, vomiting on the side of the road in a foreign country and wondering how everyone else was feeling inside the minibus when they saw what was happening to me. I wondered if they would be afraid to breathe when I got back inside. Would they be petrified of catching whatever germ it was that I was carrying? When the vomiting had settled down, I got back into the minibus, and we then carried on with our journey to the hotel.

When we arrived, I remember walking into the lobby and, after that, waking up on a bed in the hotel room. I have no recollection of how I got there. The first thing I looked for was my luggage, and it was safe with me in the room. The whole thing seemed like a dream. How could I not remember anything from when I entered the hotel lobby to being in the hotel room? I felt so confused! I continued to lie on the bed and eventually dozed off into la-la land.

When I woke up, I needed to get to the toilet in a hurry. Not only was I feeling nauseous and needed to throw up again, but by then, I had diarrhoea as well. Oh my gosh, this was insane! After cleaning myself up, I made my way back to the bed and reached for the telephone to contact reception. When the receptionist answered my call, all I could say was 'I need a doctor urgently, please!' My voice was everything but chirpy, and I might even say, almost unclear. My throat was extremely dry and sore from all the stomach acid that was passing through it. I lay there, hoping and praying someone would turn up and save me. It probably wasn't long at all since I made the phone call, but for me, it felt like ages. So I called the reception desk again in search of a doctor. After the second call, it seemed like only seconds had passed when my hotel door was flung open and three people came hurrying into the room. Two of them were paramedics, and the other person was one of the hotel staff. They put me on a stretcher and took me to the ambulance that was parked outside.

Once in the ambulance, it was as if I was going in and out of consciousness. I remember the ambulance ride very vaguely, but once we arrived at the hospital, one of the male nurses put an oxygen mask on my face. Whether I had one of them on me in the ambulance or not, I can't be sure, but I presume so.

Once we arrived at the hospital, I started feeling very anxious. There was a lot of panic taking place all around me, and I knew that as I lay there, those fantastic medical staff members were doing everything they could to try and make me feel better and settle me down. A drip was inserted into my arm once again, and after taking a few blood samples from me, I was taken to the ICU ward, where everything became a lot more settling. I was given a tranquilliser drug of some sort through the drip and settled down into a lovely deep sleep.

One word of advice that I have for everyone who travels abroad is that you should always take out travel insurance. One of the first questions I was asked when I got to the hospital was 'Have you got travel insurance?' I must say that the nursing in Malaysia was absolutely amazing. Those people are absolutely dedicated to their profession. They continuously go out of their way to make the patients comfortable and happy. They have got the greatest respect for people who are not well, and when they discuss anything amongst themselves, they keep their voices down and are soft-spoken. It was actually very comforting being in the hospital. I felt a sense of security, because although I knew I was dangerously ill, I also knew I was in very good hands. The calm and peaceful atmosphere in the ward was exactly what I needed.

All the normal procedures took place—the checking of the blood sugar levels, blood pressure, and temperature, and all the medications. At that stage of my life, this was what happened to me once a year for six weeks at a time, so it was pretty much the routine for me. I must say, though, that with all the procedures that went on day after day, I felt completely exhausted. That was also nothing new, but you never quite get used to it. When I was awake, I was continuously throwing up, and the doctors and nurses eventually felt so helpless, because they just didn't know what to do with me to improve my condition.

The Australian consulate contacted Charl to let him know what had happened to me on my journey home, and Charl immediately proceeded to make arrangements to fly to Malaysia to be with me. However, because his passport needed to be updated, it took a few days before he was issued a new one. In the meantime, he got hold of Chez and asked her if she could go to Malaysia to visit me in the hospital. My hubby was extremely concerned and wanted her to go to make sure I was all right, because he knew she would be able to get there before he could. He paid for her aircraft ticket, and being the good friend anyone could wish for, she immediately put her personal life on hold and was on her way the very next day. What an amazing man! He's the loving, supportive husband every woman dreams of having.

It was very exciting to learn that Chez was on her way to see me. The nurses let me know about her planned arrival on the next day, and oh my goodness, did that do a whole lot for me! I had something great to look forward to.

I must say, though, that I was very impressed with the Australian government. One of the nurses came over to my bedside and handed me a telephone. She told me somebody wanted to talk to me. I thought it might be Charl, but then there was a strange voice on the other side of the line. A lady from the Australian consulate introduced herself to me and started asking me a few questions. She wanted to know if I was happy with the way I was being treated in the hospital in that country.

She asked me a few other questions too, one of them being, was there anything I had requested in the hospital that had not been given to me? I was absolutely mind-blown that someone in the government department in Australia was concerned about me being ill in a foreign country. I realise this is what happens to anyone who travels overseas, but as I had not had this happen to me before, it was a huge surprise! It makes you feel very special, and it makes you love your country even more than you already did before. I do believe it was that incident that made me embrace even more the fact that Australia was our new home. I assured her I was being given the best of all treatments possible. The nurses and doctors made me feel like a VIP.

Another good thing that happened during the conversation was the fact that the nausea and vomiting seemed to be giving me a rest. I experienced what it was like not to feel ill. Unfortunately, that only lasted for approximately fifteen minutes, until the phone call had ended.

On the following day, I had some unexpected visitors. They were staff members who were from the hotel I was meant to be staying in. If they hadn't been dressed in uniform, I would not have known who they were. There was a lady and two gentlemen, and they arrived, holding a beautiful large basket of fruit. Oh my gosh, that fruit looked delicious! I was amazed at my own thoughts. I couldn't believe my taste buds had woken up. Or was it just my mind playing games with me? It was the first time in two weeks since having arrived in Cape Town, South Africa, that I felt like I had an appetite again.

I was completely blown away by the fact that the hotel staff had come to pay me a visit. How exceptionally courteous and considerate is that, might I ask? One of the first questions I asked them was if they knew the whereabouts of my luggage. They had locked my luggage safely away in one of their locker rooms; most of all, it was good to know that my passport was safely locked away too, in the hotel's safe. They were such an organised group of people, but I guess they would have to be, in the line of business they were in. They told me not to worry about anything at all. All my belongings were well taken care of, which I found to be very comforting. After a while, they wished me well and said their goodbyes and then left my bedside to go back to work. I lay there in absolute amazement at the professional and caring deed that had just been carried out. It was wonderful to be able to focus on something different other than feeling ill, but that focus didn't last for very long. Before I knew it, I was back on the road—the same old nasty road to nausea and vomiting.

Every now and then, my body would be allowed to have a break from that awful feeling. During one of those times, I looked at the basket of fruit, and all I could think was that I wanted to have some fruit juice. I knew I wouldn't be able to stomach anything, but my mind went into overdrive. I lay there, looking at every single piece of fruit in the basket, and visualised drinking a glass of each one of them. I thought that if I pressed the buzzer, I could ask one of the nurses to take some of the fruit out of the basket and have it juiced for me. I still had the drip in my arm. I knew I couldn't possibly swallow anything without it charging back up my stomach and launching itself out of my mouth like a rocket, but the craving for fruit juice was intense.

I noticed the buzzer was just out of reach of my hand, and to tell you the truth, I just did not have the strength to go the extra mile to try to reach it anyway. But I somehow found the energy to put my hand into the basket and take hold of two juicy purple grapes. I did something that no educated, civilised person would do. I held the two grapes in my hand and pointed my thumb in the direction of my mouth to make a path that the grape's juices could flow along before entering my mouth. I squeezed with all my might, but all my might wasn't a whole lot of strength at all. I reckon that Mighty Mouse probably had more strength than I did at that point.

Now picture this: There is an Australian woman in a hospital bed. She is a civilised human being and speaks perfect English, but her behaviour is somewhat common, or feral, as it is commonly known in Australia.

She is squeezing grapes in the palm of her hand, and instead of using a glass or a cup, she is forcing the juice to flow down her thumb and into her mouth. I don't know if it is just me, but I would think that maybe the poor nurses who were watching the show might have had a slightly different opinion of all the ladies from Australia after that show! Most people generalise, so I wouldn't be surprised if they lost sleep over what they had just seen or if they suffered from nightmares for a few nights. LOL! I must have looked like I had come out of the jungle. On the other hand, they might have laughed for days afterwards.

The next thing I knew, one of the nurses had come over to me with a wet facecloth to wipe my face and hands. She then took the squashed grapes away from me. Well, that just broke my heart. Why did she have to take my grapes away from me? I was really enjoying them! Did she not realise, first, how hard I had worked to get hold of them and, second, how much effort I had put into squeezing them until I was able to get a drink from them? I was completely emotionally and physically drained at that point, and my emotions got the better of me. Who has ever cried over two grapes being taken away from them? Well, I did! I must have cried myself to sleep, because I suddenly woke up and noticed that my entire fruit basket had been taken away from me. That added to the extremity of my depressed state of mind.

The days passed, and it was on the fifth day that I decided to throw in the towel and give up on life once again. I had obviously experienced this feeling before, but there I was, back in that very dark place that I never ever wanted to be in again. All I wanted out of life at that stage was to have my husband, my two children, and our two little dogs, Benjamin and Rocky, at my side. But instead of having all that, all I had was a hospital bed that was in a hospital that didn't have fresh fruit, and the breakfast menu consisted of clear soup with a touch of some spice or other that just didn't satisfy the taste buds at all. Oh gosh, my life was never meant to be this way. I was losing a lot of weight once again, which was fine with me, but the circumstances just weren't worth that weight loss at all.

I can fully understand how some people want to end their lives. I had reached a point where I could not tolerate the thought of taking one more breath. I was sick of being sick, sick of not being able to eat or drink, sick of being attached to the drip, sick of not seeing my family and friends, and just plain sick of everything and everyone. Wow, that's a whole lot of negativity coming from me right there, but that is exactly how I was feeling. Please, somebody, pull the plug on me! I didn't want to exist like that anymore! The lovely nurses kept on trying to encourage me to get up out of the bed and go for a walk down the passage, but I was also sick of hearing them trying to motivate me. Could they not see how ill I was? I just wanted to be left alone and pass on to the next life. The nurses were amazed at the fact that all I did day and night was sleep. They used to ask me if I wanted to read anything, but I wasn't interested in doing anything at all. I just wanted to be left alone so that I could peacefully pass away.

Then one night, one of the nurses came over to my bedside and told me she had some good news for me. Good news? Did such a thing even exist in my very dark, sickly world? She told me my friend Chez was on her way to visit me from Australia. She would be arriving in the morning. That was a huge energy boost! I believe I was able to put a smile on my normally very sad face. I was surprised my face didn't crack. I hadn't smiled in more than two weeks. The excitement was overwhelming. I wanted to go into space and push the Earth so that it revolved around the sun at a much quicker pace. Couldn't it travel any faster?

On the following morning, I heard the most beautiful sound that I had been looking forward to hearing. It was the lively, spunky voice of my friend Chez. She walked into the ward, and her first words to me were 'Hell, my friend, now you have me flying across the flipping world to visit you in the hospital. Your husband phoned me and told me to pack a suitcase because I would be flying to Kuala Lumpur ASAP to visit you. So here I am. Hurry up and get better, because I want you to be able to fly back home with me. I'll be here for three days.'

Seeing Chez's face and hearing her voice was one of the best things that could have happened to me on that day. I felt a sense of feeling at home, although I was nowhere near home. That girl is hysterically funny! She is always able to make me laugh, even when things seem so dull. I lay there, listening to her talk, and I don't think I stopped smiling and even laughing during the entire time she was sitting at my bedside. I really enjoyed Chez's company, but she eventually had to go back to the hotel. She told me she would see me again later on in the afternoon. After she left, I lay in bed, thinking about how she had gotten me to lighten up the first time, when I was in the hospital in Australia.

When she returned, she told me that she had enjoyed a lovely lunch and that she had had a glass of guava juice to drink. Oh my gosh, when she mentioned the guava juice, I suddenly had yet another craving for fruit juice. Not just any juice this time. It had to be guava juice!

Chez stayed for a while and then told me she was going to go back to the hotel room again and would visit me the following day. I do believe she was suffering from jet lag.

The next morning, when she arrived, I told her I was craving guava juice after having heard her talk about it, so she went off to have a chat with the nurses about fixing me a glass. Unfortunately, there wasn't any guava juice available, but she was able to arrange for me to have a glass of orange juice to sip. It went down extremely well, and then I suddenly realised my stomach had accepted the drink and had not thrown it right back up at me. Was that possible? Was I getting well?

Chez's stay for the three days seemed to have gone very quickly, and then she had to leave to return to Australia. Unfortunately, I was still not well enough to fly home, so I stayed in the hospital and was very sad to see her go. I hadn't gone for a walk in over a week, and with the tremendous weight loss that had occurred and the fact that my muscles were not getting any exercise, I was extremely weak. So once again, I withdrew into that dark place and lay on the bed, wishing that by some miracle or other, I would be up and about and living my life to the full again, but at the same time not believing it was possible for that to happen. Fortunately for me, I was in for yet another surprise. As I lay in the bed, feeling as if I was doomed to live in the hospital for the rest of my life, one of the nurses came up to me and told me my husband would be in Kuala Lumpur in three days' time. Wow, now that was also something to be over the moon about!

Exactly three days later, I heard the sweet, loving, and kind voice of my husband as he was making his way to the room. When he saw me, he was amazed at how terribly thin I was again. He said I looked like a skeleton, and when I lifted my arms to give him a hug, my muscles looked flat. After a while, Charl told me to get out of the bed so that I could try and walk around the ward with him at my side, but I simply didn't have the strength to do so. He then requested a wheelchair from one of the nurses and told me to get out of the bed and get into it, which I also didn't want to do. He insisted that I do what he was asking me to do, so with his help, I ended up sitting in the wheelchair. Then he took me on a scenic tour of the hospital ward.

It's so strange how the smallest of things in life can be so meaningful. It was very entertaining being able to see a different part of the hospital ward, even though it looked just like the part I was in. I felt a boost of excitement and hope whilst we were out there on our 'scenic tour'.

When we got back to my bed, Charl told me to put effort into walking around the ward, no matter how difficult it was for me. He spent the entire day at the hospital with me and ended up talking to one of the doctors and told him this illness was not new to us, as it seemed to happen every year, between the months of April and May. He told the doctor that he should contact the first hospital I was in, in Australia. Dr Drake would also be able to send him my file, which contained my medical history. The doctor agreed to do so. An email was sent from Australia that explained what medication was previously used to help me, but in saying that, the email the doctor in Malaysia sent to the doctor in Australia stated I had diabetic **ketoacidosis**.

We had no idea what the meaning of **ketoacidosis** was! This was the first time we had heard it being mentioned. I have got some advice in this regard. It would be a good idea to always have a folder in your luggage that states your medical history, together with your doctor's contact details and the contact details of any hospitals you might have been admitted to in the past.

I was treated immediately, and good results were showing at a rate of knots. Within two days' time, the nausea and vomiting started easing off, and I was starting to feel better again. In fact, I was starting to feel fantastic! All that was then left for me to do was to get out of the bed and start using my muscles again. I knew I had to apply myself; otherwise, I could visualise Charl having to leave for Australia without me. Emotions were running high. Charl spent the whole day with me, but when he left to go back to his hotel room that night, one of the nurses came over to me to have a chat. She explained to me that if I was not able to get up and go for a walk around the ward, I would not be released from the hospital. She told me that Charl had planned to take me back to the hotel with him the next morning. It was meant to be a surprise, but thankfully, she realised she had to tell me about the plan in order to encourage me.

I'll tell you what—I must have got a double dose of adrenaline, because somehow I managed to drag myself out of the bed and used the walls as a means of support so that I didn't end up falling to the ground. I was on a mission to impress the nurses. I noticed they were watching me, so I put every ounce of energy into each step I took. I wanted it to look like I was coping just fine, but anybody could see how much I was struggling. The main thing was that I was putting in a lot of effort.

On the following morning, Charl and I waited anxiously for the doctor to let us know if I could be discharged from the hospital. The doctor did a final examination on me, and then came the best news ever. He was happy to let me go. There were conditions attached to my leaving the hospital though. Firstly, we had to upgrade our aircraft tickets from economy class to business class, and secondly, we had to stay in Kuala Lumpur for the next five days, until a doctor had re-examined me to see if I was fit enough to fly home.

We updated our plane tickets to business class, which cost us an extra 1,000 AUD, but that was okay. We had to do what was requested of us. Those things had to be done before the doctor would give me his approval to leave Malaysia.

I must point out how beautiful the hotel was. I couldn't believe the fact that when I had arrived at the hotel on my way back from South Africa and went to my room, I hadn't seen any of what I was noticing now. The service was excellent, and the food was to die for (just saying). Oh, and might I say, I ended up having a few glasses of guava juice too during our stay. I thoroughly enjoyed the use of their room service, because I was then able to enjoy delicious meals whilst watching movies on the TV channels.

Because my muscles were extremely weak, it felt as if I was learning to walk again, but being out of the hospital environment and having my husband with me, I had the strength and the desire to get well again. I remember how shocked I was to see my body in the mirror. I certainly did look like a skeleton!

As each day passed, I started feeling a lot stronger, and I had picked up on my walking pace too. At first, I was as slow as a snail, but I eventually reached the stage where I could almost keep up with Charl.

My husband was an absolute gem! Not only did he show me so much love, but he took me for walks throughout the hotel. On the ground floor, there were a few shops I could have a look at. The one shop I enjoyed the most had all sorts of knick-knacks and goodies in it. My eyes were drawn to a beautiful bracelet with the most exquisite pink cubic zirconias. My heart melted when I looked at it, and the next thing I knew, Charl had taken it to the lady at the till and bought it for me. I looked at that gorgeous piece of jewellery on my arm and thought how lovely it was to be able to wear it. It was so sparkly. I had been in such a dull headspace over the past month, and it felt magnificent to be living out in the fresh air and living a normal life again.

I noticed my vision had become very blurry, and I had to wear my glasses to be able to see all the items in the shops clearly. I only noticed that once I was out of the hospital, so I had to wear my glasses most of the time whilst living at the hotel with Charl. Thankfully though, over time, the problem went away, and I was able to see clearly again. I was extremely concerned at the time that I might have been going blind.

When Charl noticed I was regaining my strength, he started taking me for walks in the streets. We went to the markets and browsed through all the different sweets, drinks, clothing, ornaments, and everything else you can think of. I found it so interesting and enjoyable. I could think of nothing better at the time than being with my husband in a foreign country and staying in a beautiful hotel and having all our meals prepared for us. Having our room cleaned was also wonderful. It started to feel as if we were on holiday. I did have to be careful though. I had to keep in mind that my body was extremely fragile and very unfit, but you know that feeling when you just want to keep on going? It was a great feeling to have the will to want to live again after I had been down in the dumps for such a long time. My husband made my stay in Kuala Lumpur very enjoyable once I was out of the hospital. He definitely lit the fire in my soul, and I was on the road to recovery once again. It felt very special indeed when the hotel staff commented on how happy they were to see I was feeling well again.

The day had finally come for us to board the plane and head back home to Australia. Just for the record, I had never flown business class before. I was very impressed with how much better the seating and all the services on the plane were, in comparison to flying economy class. I could then come to terms with the amount of money we had to pay for me to fly back home in comfort.

When we boarded the aircraft, one of the air hostesses approached us, and we were surprised to see that she knew our names. We were offered champagne before take-off. There was so much space all around us when we were seated, and the cutlery and crockery was stainless steel and porcelain. The toilet was even a bit fancy, with a small bouquet of flowers situated on the basin shelf. The VIP treatment was most welcome, and I rate the flight all the way home at the highest level. The airline we chose to fly with was Malaysia Airlines. I'm sure there are millions of you people out there who have had the same experience as we had. I'll be quite happy to use the airline again any time we decide to go overseas.

During the flight, the air hostesses continuously checked on me to see if I was all right. They knew I was a diabetic who was quite fragile at that stage, and they even asked me if I had taken my insulin before I started eating the meals that were served. I was highly impressed with their services.

It was a great feeling when we landed at the Brisbane International Airport and even better when we took off from the domestic terminal and landed in our home town. After being away from my children for four weeks, it was the most amazing feeling to see the two of them again. The house felt so warm when I walked in. We were finally at home again. The greeting I received from our children and our little dog Benjamin was something no amount of money could ever buy. It was another one of the most precious moments in my life. I was very impressed with how well the children had coped whilst Charl and I were overseas. The house was immaculately clean, the garden was well kept, and Benjamin looked as if he had enjoyed his meals. The kids looked as if they had grown taller and even seemed to have matured a little. All I can say is that the saying 'There is no place like home' is so true to its word!

It wasn't long before I was back to my normal self again, getting stuck in the day-to-day chores of doing all the housework, going grocery shopping, etc. Routine became part of my life again, and I am very happy to say that from then on, Charl and the kids were able to focus on their everyday commitments without having to focus on mine as well.

WHAT I HAVE LEARNT

Ketoacidosis is a serious condition. It is associated with very high blood glucose levels in **Type 1** diabetes. It develops gradually over hours or days. It is an indication that there is not enough insulin in the body, and can develop over a matter of hours or days.

The body's cells need enough insulin to use glucose for energy. Because of the lack of insulin, the body has to burn fat instead. Dangerous chemical substances accumulate in the blood, which are called ketones. They also appear in the urine. Some of the symptoms are dehydration, vomiting, and a fruity odour in the breath.

This is a serious medical condition and can be life-threatening if it is not treated properly. If you have these symptoms, it is a good idea to contact your doctor immediately or go straight to the hospital for treatment and observations.

CHAPTER 6

TWO GUARDIAN ANGELS

The rest of the year went very well. I felt fit and healthy, and my blood sugar readings ranged between 7 and 10 on average, which is still a bit high, but not as high as they had been in the past. I was happy to be able to spend Christmas with my family that year. After the terrible experience in South Africa and Malaysia, I was extremely careful about what I had to eat and drink, and I told myself I didn't ever want to end up in that situation again; even on Christmas day, I only had a small taste of the Christmas cake. I stuck to the lean meat, which was corned beef, and only ate the white meat of the chicken and not the skin, which contains fat. I felt quite proud of myself and went home feeling like, after resisting all the temptation treats of Christmas Day, I was well on the road to never having to go back to the hospital again.

As the days and months passed, my sugar readings started getting high again. I started eating the wrong foods. It's that simple! **BAM**-CFS!!!!! I would give myself a good shot of insulin to bring the sugar levels down, and before I knew it, I would then be in need of sugar again, because my sugar level would drop too low. And so the roller-coaster ride started again. Too high, then too low. This went on month after month, and I started feeling like I was fighting a losing battle again. I started going into a state of depression.

I was always worried about what was going on inside my body. As a diabetic, you should always have some form of sugar or glucose with you at all times to help you along if you end up having low sugar. I knew that and always did that, but even that was becoming an issue for me. I just wanted to be able to go for long walks, go shopping, and do sporting activities without having to make sure I had something sugary with me in case of a low. The other frustration I was finding hard to deal with was the fact that I always had to carry a bottle of water around with me everywhere I went and a bottle of juice or fizzy drink. My shoulders started aching from having to carry all that weight around with me in my handbag.

I started feeling that I was not in control of my blood sugar levels anymore, and eventually I started suffering from anxiety attacks. I knew I had to make an appointment to see my doctor. After talking to her and telling her how I was feeling, she suggested I see a diabetic educator. She gave me a referral, and I managed to get an appointment to see one a few days later.

After I talked to her for a while and answered her questions, she said something to me that made me very angry. One of her questions was 'How many times a day do you test your blood sugar readings?' My reply was 'About six to eight times a day'. She wanted to know why I did it that many times, and then I told her the reason for that was that I needed to know what my blood sugar reading was throughout the entire day. I didn't think it was okay when she told me she thought I needed to see a psychiatrist! She said there must be underlying issues with me that made me want to check my blood so many times a day. I was shocked at what she said, because it is quite normal to do that many readings on a daily basis. I'd say I was doing a good job. At least I wasn't only checking my blood sugar readings once or twice a day. If anything, I would have thought she would be satisfied with what I had said, because in one of the diabetic diaries I use, there are eight blocks for you to fill in your daily readings. Anyway, look, things happen in life, and I put that day behind me and moved on.

It was only a few days later, and I was at home, busy cooking dinner for Charl and myself, when I started feeling slightly nauseous. Could this really be happening? It certainly was. I told Charl I wasn't feeling well, and he told me we should probably go to the hospital. That was the last place I wanted to be. I did, after all, promise myself I would never end up going there again. I told him I just needed to lie down and relax, because I had been under a lot of stress and I thought it was getting the better of me. After I had dished up Charl's dinner, I lay down on the bed and prayed the nausea would go away. But my prayer was not answered, and the vomiting started again. It went on for most of the night, and by the next morning, Charl and I were on our way to the hospital.

This pattern had become so regular, and when we arrived at the hospital, I was admitted immediately. By that time, I was extremely dehydrated and was put on the intravenous drip straight away. I wasn't able to keep water down, but my mouth was so dry one of the nurses gave me some ice to suck on. Oh, good grief, vomit bags became my best friends once again. It was awful. Everything that happened in the hospital was a repetition of all my previous stays.

As I lay on the bed, I wondered if that was going to be the end of the road for me. Throughout every single year, I felt great, but as soon as April or May arrived, I was almost guaranteed to be admitted into the hospital. The nausea and vomiting got very bad, as was normally the case, and then one of the hospital's doctors gave the nurses instructions to have me transferred to ICU. My condition remained a mystery; because I was getting ill at the same time each year, the doctors were considering the cause of the problem to be seasonal. In other words, they were suspicious that my illness could have something to do with the weather.

All procedures carried on as normal—the monitoring of blood pressure, temperature, blood sugar readings, etc. It was impossible for me to eat anything. After being in ICU for just a few hours, another patient was wheeled into the ward as well. The patient was an old lady. She must have been in her late sixties or early seventies. I wasn't sure what was going on with her, as the curtain was drawn while the nurses worked with her. She was, however, calling out and telling them to stop whatever they were doing to her. It was obvious they were trying to help her, but she wasn't seeing it that way. After a lot of struggle, she quietened down, and the ward was peaceful again. After a short while, the dear old lady fell asleep, while the rest of us had to listen to her snoring. Fortunately, though, the old lady was removed from ICU in the morning and was taken downstairs to the general ward.

After the doctors had paid me a visit, I could hear the sound of the food trolley heading towards our ward. I couldn't stand the thought of food, and I carried on with feeling nauseous and vomiting. I couldn't help but wonder how the other patients were feeling when they constantly heard me throwing up. I tried to keep the tone down as best as I could, but it was obvious what I was doing. A tray consisting of a bowl of oats, a glass of orange juice, and a slice of toast with a small tub of vegemite was placed on the trolley table that slid over the bed. The sight of the breakfast meal just made my stomach turn even more. How on earth could they think I would be able to stomach food? I couldn't wait for the meal to be taken away from me, and when it was, it was a relief. I was ill for the rest of the day. When the lunchtime meal arrived, I was just as uninterested in it as I was when the breakfast meal was in front of me. The meal that night was no different.

One of the nurses had her eye on me quite a lot. It felt as if she was very interested in me. She would look at me, and whenever she was talking to one of the other nurses, regardless of which one, they would look in my direction and talk very quietly to one another. It was obvious I was the topic of discussion, and I couldn't help but wonder what she was saying each time.

The next morning, breakfast arrived again, but I still had no interest in attempting to eat it. In a short while, the nurse came over to see me. She told me that because I had lost so much weight and because there was no sign of improvement with my health, the one thing they wanted me to do was to try and start eating. She also told me that if I was not able to eat some of my breakfast, they would have to feed me in the same manner they fed the old lady who was lying next to me, and that would be by forcing the food into my body through a tube that would be inserted into my mouth and go down my throat and into my stomach. I was very weak, and they were concerned because they could see I was getting weaker by the day. They had to get food into my system somehow.

I'll tell you what, she could just as well have lit a dynamite stick and placed it next to me on the bed. I picked up the spoon and scooped up some of the oats. She stood there, watching me. I put the spoon into my mouth, and as soon as the oats came off the spoon, the vomiting motions started. I knew I couldn't afford to throw up, not with the very strict nurse standing right in front of me! Down it went, and my stomach somehow didn't refuse the oats' entry. I cringed as it slid down my throat, but when I looked up and saw the smile on the nurse's face, it was all well worth it. She looked completely satisfied, and that felt kind of rewarding.

She told me to take another mouthful of oats. Gosh, wasn't one mouthful enough? I went in for the second, third, and fourth mouthfuls, and then I knew I had to stop eating; otherwise, it was going to come straight up again, and I would find myself struggling with the nurses as they tried to force that tube down my throat. That was the first time in weeks that I had consumed anything. I was on a high! I was very pleased that I had swallowed food and that it stayed in my stomach. I really did owe all my appreciation to the cute but strict nurse. In fact, I thanked her for being a sergeant major. LOL! Fortunately for me, she did not take offence to that comment but had a bit of a giggle. I heard her telling the other nurses what I had called her, and they all found it quite funny.

Later on in the morning, Charl came to visit me. He was happy to see me smiling. I told him I had eaten three tablespoons of oats for breakfast and had kept it down. That put a huge smile on his face too. It's amazing how the little things in life that we take for granted are always so meaningful during times of struggle. I stayed in ICU for two more days after that, before I was sent back to the general ward.

When Charl came back in the afternoon to visit me again, he found out I had been moved from ICU to the general ward. He spoke to one of the doctors and asked him if my bowels had moved yet. When the doctor's reply was no, Charl told him I would be back in ICU within about two days. He knew this because of all the experience we had had in the past.

Well, lo and behold, if it didn't happen again! As I lay on the bed, I started feeling nauseous. It was unbelievable! What on earth was going on? I pressed the panic button to call one of the nurses and told her how I was feeling. She asked me if I wanted tablets for the nausea or if I wanted her to put the medication into the drip. If it wasn't for the nausea, I was certain I would not have had to remain attached to the drip. I was hoping I would be freed from it. I told her I would prefer to have the medication through the drip, as swallowing anything and keeping it down was going to be an issue once again. And so my journey in the hospital carried on. Well, as you can probably imagine, the next thing I knew, I was on my way back to ICU. Charl's prediction of me being moved back there within the next two days was spot on! I have to tell you that the doctor told Charl he realised that Charl knew quite a lot about my condition. This was due to the fact that we had gone through it so many times before.

I was happy to have had a break from it all over the past three days in ICU. I wouldn't be surprised if the nursing staff were wondering if I was going to end up dying there. To be honest, at that point, I would have been very happy to pass away. I just couldn't take it anymore! Then suddenly, out of the blue, a bubbly, pretty lady walked up to me and introduced herself. She was a diabetic educator. She had a talk with me and was just the tonic I had needed for a number of years! She asked me several questions, one of them being, if the nurses had checked my ketones. Ketones! This word was mentioned when I was in Malaysia, but we were still unaware of its meaning. She briefly explained to me what it was all about, and then she told me one of the nurses was going to check my ketones. She had to leave by then, and she told me she would be in touch with the hospital to find out what my ketone readings were.

In the meantime, Charl had turned up to visit me. While he was talking to me, a nurse came up to me and asked me to give her one of my fingers to prick again. This time, it was to check my ketones. When Charl saw the glucometer she was using, he asked her where we could get one of them. She told him the pharmacies sold them. Both of us were shocked to hear that. I had spent six weeks at a time, every year, for the past six years, in the hospital with an illness nobody could pinpoint; and after such a long time of literally coming close to death, we learnt about ketones and the ketone monitor from a diabetic educator. It was unfortunate that in all the time I suffered as much as I did, I had no knowledge of being able to check my ketones when I wasn't feeling well. We were completely in the dark and had no idea at all as to what was going on with my body. It was very surprising to know that the answer was staring us right in the face. Then suddenly, the word **ketoacidosis** came to mind, from when I was ill in the hospital in Malaysia. For the first time though, we then understood the meaning of the word, and so the doors started opening up for us.

I also used to be under the care of a diabetic specialist a long time ago, who never mentioned the word ketones. In the way that I see it, it is a very important topic that every diabetic should learn about. In this day and age, we are very fortunate to have access to the Internet, which enables us to do a lot of research on almost everything.

The day Michelle walked into the hospital and saw me was the day we finally got some answers in regard to this horrible illness that I had to live with each year. I was so grateful to Charl for asking the nurse where we could get the ketone monitor. Well, there you go. You can be a diabetic for many years, and there will always be room to learn so much more about the disease. Charl and that wonderful lady are my two guardian angels. From that day onwards, my health continued to improve whilst I was in the hospital. She must have let the doctors know what was going on with me. I have yet to ask her how she had heard about me in the first place.

Once I was discharged from the hospital, I no longer had to worry about the months of April and May coming up. I knew exactly how to take care of myself. It was such a relief not having the torment and fear of that time of the year arriving. The sad thing is that my birthday is in April, and I used to not know if I would be spending it with my family or spending it in the hospital. However, after that, life became a whole lot better, because I felt as if I had reached the point of having peace of mind.

WHAT I HAVE LEARNT

People with **Type 1** diabetes who don't take enough insulin will cause the body to start burning its own fats as a substitute which releases chemical substances in the blood. If insulin is not taken, the dangerous chemical substances will accumulate. This condition is known as **ketoacidosis**, and if left untreated can be life threatening.

CHAPTER 7

THE SECOND LAST HURDLE

In 2016, I decided to take another trip to South Africa to visit my mother, who was not well. It wasn't easy having a conversation with her on the telephone while she was feeling unwell, and because I was thousands of kilometres away from her, I felt the urgent need to go and visit her. After I had finished talking to her, I spoke to Charl and explained my concern for her, and he agreed with the idea of me going to visit her as soon as possible. So once again, I was off to the travel agency to book a plane ticket to South Africa. If only it was as simple as that this time round though. I still had three months to go before my passport was going to expire, so I wasn't at all hesitant when I approached the travel agent. It does state at the back of every Australian passport that you do have to have at least six months' availability in order for you to leave the country. I have to admit that I did not see that. So the travel agent I was dealing with immediately phoned the immigration office in Brisbane to find out what we could do to speed up the renewal of my passport.

It was going to take at least three weeks before my passport would be ready. I did not have three weeks to wait. This was an urgent matter, and I needed it as soon as possible! The only other way I could get a new passport done quickly would be for me to fly to Brisbane and go for an interview to see if an emergency passport could be arranged. I was quite happy to do that, so the travel agent booked me on a flight that would leave for Brisbane the very next morning.

The interview went well. I found the clerk to be very helpful, but there was just one problem. In order for the department to issue me with an emergency travel document, they needed a letter from my mother's doctor, stating she was in poor health. Unfortunately, there was no way I could do that. My mother is of the old school, as can be expected, and I knew she would get very frustrated and confused if I asked her for her doctor's contact details. I didn't even know her doctor's name, so I was completely in the dark. With my being there, the clerk told me they could have the new passport ready in three working days. I was happy with that. Three days was so much better than having to wait for three weeks. Because of that, I had to go back to the travel agent on Saturday morning to let her know I would need to book another plane ticket to Brisbane the following Wednesday and leave for South Africa on Thursday night. I wanted a late international booking, just in case there was a hiccup at the immigration department which could possibly make me late for my flight.

The week went by really quickly, and before I knew it, Charl and I were sitting at the airport, waiting for my call for the flight to Brisbane. Both Charl and I were very concerned about the flight, because it would mean I was potentially in danger of once again falling ill to **ketoacidosis**. I put on a brave act though and told him I would be fine. I was going to protect myself from those dreaded ketones, so when I boarded the aircraft at the Brisbane International Airport, I took two bottles of water with me, which I had to purchase at the duty-free shop at the airport, together with a box of hydrolyte sachets.

During the flight, I was constantly drinking water, and every now and then, I would add hydrolytes to the water to keep myself hydrated. We were approximately six hours into the flight when I felt the ketones moving in. My tongue got very dry, and I started feeling nauseous. All I could think was Oh no, am I getting **ketoacidosis** again?

The nausea got worse, and I eventually decided to get up out of my seat and go to the back of the plane, where I was sure to find an air hostess who could possibly help me. I told her I needed to drink a lot of water. I had drank all the water I had taken aboard the plane at take-off. She handed me a small plastic cup of water, and then I explained to her that I needed a bottle of water. She told me it was unfortunately not possible to give me a bottle of water, as the passengers were not allowed to make that request.

I explained to her that I was a diabetic and that I was in the process of getting **ketoacidosis**, so if I didn't get a bottle of water, I would be throwing up at any given moment. I told her that because I had experienced this before, once the throwing up started, I would end up in ICU in one of the hospitals in Dubai once the plane landed. She immediately handed me a bottle of water, which I thanked her for, and then I returned to my seat. I was feeling terrible, and I knew for sure that I would start throwing up soon!

Before I opened the bottle top, there was a tap on my shoulder. When I looked up, the head steward was standing next to me in the aisle. He asked me to tell him my name and then told me to follow him to the centre of the plane, where I was offered a seat. He told me my situation had become a medical incident, and he asked me a few questions and filled out the answers for me on the medical report. I was just too ill to fill the form out on my own. He then asked me if I would accept an oxygen mask, as that should help take the nausea away. I had never heard of that before, but I was willing to try anything—jump out of the plane, do three backflips, and then latch on to the plane again and pull myself inside to avoid ending up in the hospital.

The steward put the oxygen mask on my face and opened the tap. There was a second steward with me as well, who kept an eye on the oxygen tank. After approximately twenty minutes, he asked me how I was feeling out of 10, with 10 being the strongest point. When I told him I felt like I was a 5 out of 10, he said it wasn't good enough and told me to lie down on the floor. He then brought me a pillow to rest my legs on and told me it was important that my legs were kept higher than my body. I lay there for what seemed to be about an hour. When the steward removed the oxygen mask and asked me again how I was feeling out of 10, I told him I felt like I was probably a 9. He asked me if I thought I would be all right if I went back to my seat; I told him I would, so off I went.

I wasn't feeling 100 per cent well, and I could still feel the ketones churning in my blood. But I was, however, feeling so much better than before. I was worried this was going to end up in yet another case of me being in the hospital for **ketoacidosis**. Then I was served breakfast, and one of the ingredients on the tray was a small tub of yoghurt that I was very reluctant to swallow but did. The nausea seemed to go away almost immediately after eating that. The rest of the flight went well, and when we landed in Dubai, I felt well again.

The duration until the connecting flight was going to be three hours. The first thing that came to mind was to send Charl and my family in Cape Town a text message to say that I had arrived safely in Dubai, but when I switched my mobile (cell phone) on, there was no signal. I was not able to use my phone, because the phone company in Australia had not unbarred it. The annoying part was that when I went into their office to make that arrangement, the lady who attended to me told me it was not necessary to do anything to make any changes to my phone account, because it would automatically register that I was in a foreign country, but that it would still be active as normal. I found that to be weird. I had never before gone to a foreign country without having to unbar my mobile phone. I found it to be very frustrating not being able to use my phone, and I spent the rest of the travel time worrying about Charl, who was obviously worried about me, not having heard anything from me since I had left Australia. I could just imagine him wondering if I had taken ill aboard the flight and had once again been admitted to the hospital in another foreign country.

There was nothing I could do to sort out the problem, so I walked around the airport terminal, browsing around different shops. I eventually thought I'd stop and buy a magazine to read, but when I reached into my handbag to get my reading glasses out, I discovered I had forgotten to take them with me when I disembarked from the aircraft. There was only one thing left to do. I wasn't particularly hungry or thirsty but thought it would be a good idea to sit down at one of the restaurants at the airport and try and relax over a nice cappuccino. On the way there, my handbag suddenly fell to the ground. The strap had come loose. At that point, I wasn't sure if I should board the next flight! I mean, was that flight not going to fall out of the sky for some reason? So much was going wrong on that trip! Anyway, I found a coffee shop, and believe me, I was drinking the cappuccino with great care. I could just imagine choking on it just to make the story more interesting! But just to fool me, the coffee did me no harm and went all the way into my stomach without any detours, and I survived the beverage challenge!

The three hours passed, and we were once again boarding another aircraft and heading up and beyond the clouds. I was extremely impressed when one of the air hostesses approached me and told me they were aware of the fact that I had had a medical issue aboard the previous flight. So if I needed any help at all, I was not to get out of my seat and go looking for help; I was to call them by pressing the button that was situated on the panel just below the TV set. I'm very happy to say that during the flight, I was constantly approached and asked if I was feeling okay. I'm even happier to be able to say that my body behaved itself for the rest of the way to Cape Town, which was very surprising, and I loved it.

When we arrived in Cape Town, we all had to clear customs, and then came the excitement of seeing my sister Allison, who was there to meet me at the airport. She drove me to my mother's apartment, where I was meant to stay for the next two weeks. It never went as planned though. My mother had aged a great deal since the last time I had seen her, and it was wonderful seeing the happy look on her face when she saw Allison and I walking down the corridor towards her. We greeted her and then went into her little apartment and sat down to a nice cup of coffee and a chat. Allison left soon after that, and my mom and I carried on with our conversation.

On Wednesday, Thursday, and Friday, I thoroughly enjoyed my stay with my mom. I was, however, still very concerned about her. She was so thin, and I noticed she ate like a little mouse. I am aware of the fact that a lot of older people do find that they don't have the desire to eat as much as they used to in their younger days, but then at the same time, there are those who don't have a problem with it. My mother's eating habits got the better of me, and I told her I couldn't eat any meals unless she ate with me. This was not the right approach to take, being a diabetic, but I had to work out a way of encouraging her to eat. I thought I was going to die from starvation, but I had to keep going with my plan. I will say, though, that I was secretly snacking on nuts I had bought at the airport in Brisbane, to keep myself going.

During my stay, I was very pampered and spoilt by my sisters, Allison and Pat. I was lucky enough to have been able to stay at both my sisters' houses as well. I loved seeing my brother, Johan; his wife, Rose; my nephew, Sean; and his wife, Francis. I was very happy to have been able to catch up with my nieces, Kia and Caylin, as well. I also got to spend time with my other sister, Benita; her husband, John; and of course, my niece Ilana and her gorgeous little girl, Riley. I thoroughly enjoyed spending a lot of fun time with my niece Bernie. Bernie and I are very similar. We laughed and talked about the same things, and it was also lovely seeing her husband, Shaun, and her sons, Dylan and Jesse. It was also good seeing two more nieces, Jackie and Simmy. I have a big family, whom I don't see enough of. I did spend a lot of time with my sister Allison. She is one of my idols! It was awesome not being ill that time round in South Africa; therefore, I managed to spend a lot of quality time with my whole family.

One thing I do have to mention is that my sugar level readings were always 20+. I think that was because I was highly upset about my mom. I was even upset when I was having fun (if that makes any sense).

The day came when it was time to leave South Africa and head back home to Australia. I was sad to say goodbye to my family but also very excited to be going home to my husband and children. My darling sisters, Allison, Pat, and Benita, took me to the airport, where we had something to eat and drink. Just before I started eating my meal, I looked for my insulin to have an injection but realised I had left all my insulin in my sister's fridge at her house. It was too far to drive back and fetch it, so Benita and I hurried off to the pharmacy at the airport. I was fortunate enough that the pharmacist handed me a single pen that would be enough until I got back to Australia. Then came the dreaded moment of saying goodbye. I boarded the plane, and once again, I was back in the air, where I would be doing nothing but eating, drinking, and watching movies.

Once we had levelled out, an air hostess approached me and told me that if I had any issues with my health, I should let them know, because they did have oxygen tanks aboard the flight (do these words sound familiar?). Once again, I was so impressed! It was two weeks later, and the crew on this flight were aware of my medical history and condition from the previous flights. I am very pleased to say that on the flight all the way to Dubai, I had absolutely no problem with my health.

We landed in Dubai, and three hours later, I was once again on the next flight to Brisbane, Australia. Lo and behold, yet another crew member aboard the final international flight approached me with the same message. I was more than impressed at the service that was offered to me. What an amazing airline and fantastic crew members!

We finally touched down on Australian soil, and then it was a matter of clearing customs before getting to the domestic terminal, where I was to board another aircraft which would take me home, where my husband was waiting for my arrival. It was very stressful, waiting for my luggage to arrive on the conveyor belt at the international terminal in Brisbane, because there was no sign of it at all. I think what must have happened is that someone must have taken my suitcase instead of theirs, because after a long while, my suitcase came along. They must have realised their mistake and replaced mine for theirs. It wasn't long, and we were in the air again. The excitement of getting closer to home was mind-boggling.

The only way I can describe my feelings when I saw Charl is 'What a beautiful sight!' I was home and felt safe. No more wondering if my ketones were going to surprise me while I was flying around the skies. It was also great seeing my daughter, Carrin, when she came for a visit that night, along with Charl Jnr, my son, and Shaye, his fiancée. I brought them each a gift from South Africa, which they loved!

WHAT I HAVE LEARNT

Diabetes can double a person's risk of early death. It can affect any part of your body such as your eyes, feet, legs, hands, arms, kidneys, heart, and etc. If diabetics have control over the blood sugar levels, most of these problems can be avoided.

To help control blood sugar levels, eating healthy meals, doing physical activities, and taking care of your blood pressure and cholesterol levels is important.

CHAPTER 8

JUST WHEN I THOUGHT THAT I WOULD NEVER SEE A HOSPITAL AGAIN

From the time I had come back from visiting my family in South Africa in October 2016, up until March 2017, I led a normal life. I had no issues with diabetes, and life was just great. We were two weeks into April, and there was still no sign of the dreaded **ketoacidosis**. Was I going to escape the clutch of the disease's hands? I was quite anxious, as you can well imagine, because the anniversary months hadn't completely passed yet. I tried to convince myself I had made it halfway through April without any signs of having to book into the hospital, so maybe, just maybe, I was going to get away with it this time.

One Sunday morning, Charl was having a look on the Internet at properties that were going for sale. We are both very keen to move from our present house, which is on 2.5 acres of land, to a much bigger property that consists of at least 100 acres of land. This is one of our dreams, and we are hoping that someday we will be able to fulfil that dream. After noticing a property that was situated in a small town which was not too far from where we lived, we got into the car and went for a drive to have a look at it. Whilst we were travelling on the road, Charl said it was about time for me to check into the hotel again. He said I was due for my next vacation. He was talking about me being admitted into the hospital again. He nicknamed the hospital the Hospital Inn. It became a standard joke between us, and we chatted and giggled about it for a while. I was feeling fabulous, so it was easy to joke about it.

When we arrived at the property, we drove through the gate and up to the shed that had been used as the owner's house. We had made previous arrangements with the estate agent to enter the property. It was beautiful. The shed was situated on high ground and looked down over a valley. We could see cattle in the distance that belonged to the neighbouring farmer. If there was ever going to be a flood, we would be safe. The water would not reach the house. It seemed like the perfect set-up for us. We could not see the nearest neighbour's house, and that was exactly what we wanted. With all that land available to us, Charl and I could go on bush drives in his buggy, and I could ride my horse and take the dogs for long bush walks. It was perfect for us. We stayed there for a very long time, dreaming of what could be if we bought it. We did have two problems though. We owned two houses; we would either have to sell them first before buying another property or put both houses on the rental market. We eventually decided to head back home, and we had so much to talk about along the way.

On the way home, we decided to stop at a bakery in one of the little towns to buy some treats for dinner. We bought delicious beef curry pies, and for a sweet treat, we bought apple turnovers. **BAM** – CFS!!!!! You know how it goes. Every now and then, you crave a sweet treat and anything that is naughty to eat, like the pies, for example. It was about six p.m. by the time we got home, and we sat down to our very tasty dinner. After we had finished eating, I washed the dishes and tidied up the kitchen, while Charl went for a shower and then relaxed in front of the TV set. I had my shower too after I had finished cleaning the kitchen, and I went to the bedroom to watch my weekly Sunday night TV programmes.

While I was sitting on the bed and enjoying one of my favourite shows, I started feeling ill. It was none other than the dreaded nausea, and I regretted eating so much junk food for dinner. Because I knew how to deal with the situation, I got out of bed and fetched a bottle of water. I drank it very quickly, because I knew how important it was to get as much water into my system as possible. Three bottles of water later, the floodgates opened. By that, I mean the vomiting had started again. I threw up all through the night, and by morning, I was a wreck. Charl told me to pack a bag, because he was taking me to the hospital. I knew by the tone of his voice that there was no need to debate the matter. I also knew it was the obvious thing to do, but the thought of going there again just turned my gut even more. You always hope the problem will go away by itself, but that is really just a dream. Once it sets in, you're stuck between a rock and a hard place. I had a shower and packed a bag, and we were off to the local hospital again.

When we arrived, I was admitted straight away, and the nurses and doctors who were on duty were wonderful. There weren't a lot of outpatients at the time, so it felt as if I had them all to myself. It wasn't long, and I was hooked up to the dreaded drip once again. As you already know, I can't stand being attached to that thing, and the preparation for it is a nightmare! The thought of the needle being inserted into my vein just makes me cringe. My veins are very shy. They like to hide away, which makes it so much harder for the nurses to work with, and it turns me into a nervous wreck.

After a long time, I was finally hooked up and was very carefully monitored. My ketone reading was 4, and my potassium count was low. So the nurses were treating me through the drip. After being monitored until about four-thirty that afternoon, I was feeling so much better. The nausea and vomiting had stopped, and I was able to eat a sandwich and drink a cup of tea. We were told that they wanted me to spend the night at the hospital for observations, so I thought I would probably be discharged the next day, which would be Tuesday. When I was stable, I was taken up to the ward where I was to stay for the night. Charl went home and was going to come back the following morning to fetch me and take me home.

As I lay in the bed, thinking of how quickly the medical team managed to conquer what had happened and comparing it to all the other times I had been in various hospitals, there was a knock on my door again. My visitor decided to come back! I rang the buzzer for a nurse to bring me a vomit bag, and from then on, that was what I did all day long. When Charl came to visit me, it was apparent I was not going to be leaving the hospital for a while, and so I prepared myself for a very long stay again. I guessed I would be staying there for at least another six weeks. Feeling very despondent, I felt myself withdrawing into that dark place again.

Now I know I spoke about eating those delicious bakery treats, but at the time, I also had an irritating cough. I was tested for allergies and throat infections, because the doctor thought that might have triggered the **ketoacidosis**. Since then, I have also learnt from my diabetic educator that the ketones in the body build up over time, so they don't necessarily build up overnight; when they reach a certain level, you get violently ill. This was obviously the case with me.

As quickly as it had returned, it disappeared again. I was sick all Tuesday, but by Wednesday morning, the illness had gone away. I was very confused as to what was going on. This had never happened before. It was great that I was feeling well again, but this wasn't the normal pattern. I was feeling so good that I even ordered lunch. After I ate lunch and dinner on Wednesday and breakfast on Thursday morning, one of the nurses spoke to the doctor, who gave her permission to free me from the drip. I still had the needle (cannula) in my vein, just in case I started vomiting again.

I enjoyed my stay in the hospital on Thursday. I had two visitors: Wendy, one of my dear friends, and Carrin, my lovely daughter. It felt good to be able to talk and smile again, and my hopes were high that I would be going home on Friday morning. I did notice something though, and that was that when my blood sugar levels were tested and if the readings were good—for example, under 10—the nurses would not give me an insulin injection. I knew, however, that if I did not have that shot, my blood sugar would rise considerably. I mentioned that to one of the nurses, whose response was that she was following the doctor's instructions. But when it was time to test my blood sugar readings again, which would be two hours later, my readings had gone sky-high. It was a 'huff and a puff, and I'll blow your house down' situation! That was how I felt.

There was urgent need to lower the sugar levels again, and the whole thing just seemed to go around in circles. I then asked one of the nurses if I would be allowed to give myself my own injections. I had my kit with me, so it would be very easy to do so. She came back to me with a negative answer. So after my blood sugar tests and before I ate any food, I injected the insulin I had with me in my kit into my body and then ate the meal that was in front of me. As a result, when it was time to check my blood sugar reading again, it was good.

I told them what I had been doing so that they would realise how important it was for me to have the injection before a meal, even when the blood sugar reading was below 10. The nurse obviously discussed the matter with the doctor, and she came back to me and told me that from then on, I was allowed to do all my blood sugar monitoring and all my injections on my own. They would ask me each time what my readings were and how much insulin I had taken so that they could still keep a record of all of it. I found that that worked very well for me, and my sugar levels were behaving themselves. It was always under 10, which was fantastic! I found it very easy, keeping my blood sugar readings constant, with me just lying in the hospital bed and not being active.

On Friday, at 2 a.m., one of the nurses woke me up from a deep sleep to check my blood sugar levels. I had a low reading of 2.4. I have never seen anybody panic so much in my life. In a very flustered way, she told me she would be back in a minute. When she came back, she opened a tube of GlucoGel. She told me to consume the entire tube and brought it close to my mouth and started squeezing the tube. As soon as I got the taste, I pulled my head back and told her I didn't want anymore of it. She was pretty insistent that I swallow all the contents of the tube, but I refused to do so. I pointed out the juice box that was on the table beside me, and I told her that was all I needed to drink to bring my sugar level up again.

She was very concerned and walked away for a few seconds before coming back again. She then took my hand and told me she was going to do another blood sugar test. I couldn't see why, as she had pricked my finger only a few minutes before. I let her do what she wanted to do, and then she told me it was good that my sugar level had increased to 2.7. Because I refused to take the glucose, she offered me a sandwich instead, which I thoroughly enjoyed. She told me she would return in five minutes, which was what she did. She then pricked my finger again and saw that the blood sugar level had increased even more. She then told me she would be back in the next five minutes. I watched the time, and she was spot on. When she wanted to prick my finger again, I refused to let her do it. I told her it wasn't necessary to prick my finger so many times at such short intervals. This was obviously the protocol, but it wasn't okay for me.

About half an hour later, another nurse came to see me and also wanted to take a blood sugar reading. It was a comfortable 6. I do appreciate the fact that the nurses were doing their job and were just taking good care of me. I know what it feels like to have a sugar low. I've had a few of them over the years, and I have learnt how to deal with them. After I had eaten the sandwich, I had to give myself another dose of insulin to stop my blood sugar levels from rising too high again. I kept that injection a secret until breakfast time, because it would have started the whole cycle of checking my blood all over again. I knew, though, that I would be okay, and I lay back and went to sleep.

In the morning, when the doctors did their rounds, I was told I would not be discharged from the hospital that day because of the sugar low that happened at 2 a.m. I could not believe what I was hearing. One sugar low was all it was. Other than that, I felt great. The doctor told me they wanted to keep me in the hospital for more observations. I felt frustrated! Could this really be happening? I felt as if I could end up staying in the hospital for the rest of my life.

While I was lying in the bed in disbelief of what was going on, the hospital diabetic educator came to see me. She was also under the impression I was going to be going home that day, but I told her the plan had been changed. I explained to her how the doctor had decided to keep me there for observations because of the sugar low that I had at 2 a.m. She was surprised with what she had heard. The reason for that was that she understood that every now and then, diabetic patients do have lows. She told me she would arrange for me to be discharged from the hospital the following day, which she did. I was so grateful to her. The hospital doctor explained to me that the reason I had to remain in the hospital was that if I was released and something happened to me on the way home after having had a sugar low the night before, the hospital could be held responsible. I fully understood the reason then.

During my stay that week, we had a lot of rain. In fact, it rained so much that we were having floods. I managed to catch up on all the news in regard to the floods, via the Internet on my mobile phone, but I wanted to be home again with my family. I needed to know that my husband, my horse, and my two little dogs were all safe at home.

Charl turned up to fetch me on Saturday morning, and I was thrilled to be with my family again. I hope and pray that I will escape a visit to the Hospital Inn again next year.

WHAT I HAVE LEARNT

Ketone Testing

Levels below 0.6 (all values are in millimoles per litre) are considered normal levels.

Levels 0.6 to 1.5 are considered moderate and levels.

Levels 1.6 to 3.0 are considered high levels

Low Potassium

Potassium is vital to the proper functioning of nerve and muscle cells, particularly heart muscle cells. Normally, your blood potassium level is 3.6 to 5.2 (all values are in millimoles per litre). A low potassium level less than 2.5 can be life-threatening and requires urgent medical attention.

CHAPTER 9

ARE YOU KIDDING ME!

When you turn fifty, you receive a bowel cancer test kit in the mail, wherein you give them a sample of your poo, and that gets sent away for analysis to see if you have any traces of bowel cancer. This gets sent to you every five years. Well, the time had come for me to have my second bowel cancer test done. The kit arrived in the mail, and I simply ignored it. I received two reminder letters, and Charl asked me if I had sent a sample. Eventually I decided to do so.

After sending the samples, I received a text message from my doctor's rooms, saying that she needed to see me. I arrived at the medical centre, and it wasn't long before I was called in to see her. She started with her general discussion about my health and then asked me if I had received any information regarding my test results. I wasn't sure, as I had not checked for mail in a while. Then she told me she had, and the results came back positive. It was necessary for me to have a CAT scan first, to see if there were any traces of cancer on the outside of my bowel and other parts of my internal organs. She did stipulate though that at times, some of her patients had the same positive results, but there was no cancer present. It could have meant that on the day you gave a poo sample, there might have been blood present, as a result of bleeding piles (haemorrhoids) or anything else.

I felt quite strange when I left her room. The fact that I could possibly have cancer tore me apart, as I'm sure it does with anyone who has experienced the same results. She had told me to remain positive until we knew for sure what the results were. My husband was a victim of prostate cancer, so I know what it does to entire families. Fortunately for us though, he had all of it removed and is still alive and well. I literally thank God for that.

I was then faced with the task of having to tell my family what I had just heard, and then of course, my close friends. Everyone was very worried, but I put on a brave face (as you do). For the first two days, I walked around the house like a zombie. I couldn't function properly, until I started realising I could not possibly let this problem suppress me anymore. I had been dealing with sugar diabetes for the past twenty-six years and have survived up until the present date, so I wasn't going to let this problem get the better of me. I also had to remind myself that my doctor had told me not to be too concerned because we weren't sure at that point about the outcome of the results. Stress and concern also seem to throw my blood sugar readings out of whack, so that was another reason to remain calm about the situation.

Three days later, I was back at the doctor's rooms to hear what the results of the CAT scan were. They came back negative, which was fantastic news! My doctor still wasn't completely convinced I was in the clear, because I was bleeding from somewhere. She wanted to find out where it was coming from, so she booked me into the hospital to have a colonoscopy. Millions of people have had this procedure, and that is all good and well; but as a diabetic, let me tell you what wasn't so acceptable about the pre-procedure appointment.

I received a phone call from a nurse. She had a chat with me and wanted to book an interview date so that we could have a discussion about the procedure. She also needed to know beforehand what medications I was on. Unfortunately, it was round about that time I was leaving for South

Africa to visit my mother, so I told her I would call her again to book an appointment once I got back from South Africa.

Once I was back at home, I phoned the hospital and asked to speak to her. It was late in the afternoon, and I was told that her shift had already ended. I was told that the staff did not take messages and that I should call again the following day in order to talk to her, but before I got round to doing that, she phoned me instead. We had a chat, and an appointment was made for me to see her.

I arrived on that day, and it didn't take long at all before I was called in to have my pre-procedure appointment. I was called into her room, she introduced herself, and then the discussion began. She asked me a few questions, one of them being if I had ever had a procedure of this nature or any other nature before. I told her I had had cataracts removed from one of my eyes, and I had also had my gall bladder removed. Then followed the question that often gets asked whenever I have an appointment to see a doctor. She said, 'I see that you are a diabetic! How are your sugar readings? Have you got them under control?' I explained to her that my sugar readings fluctuate at times, but that whilst I was in South Africa, I didn't have them under control at all.

On that day, my sugar level was very high too. When I had pricked my finger in the morning, the reading was 20, which is way too high, as we all know. She wanted to check my blood sugar reading on the spot; out came her glucometer, and she pricked my finger. The reading was still the same. I'll tell you what. From that moment on, she seemed to have forgotten about the reason I was actually sitting at her desk. Oh my goodness! She only spoke about diabetes and nothing else. She told me she knew of someone who was close to her that was a diabetic too, and she said that for that reason, she knew everything about the disease.

She told me that I should not inject any insulin into my body during the fasting time, which was to be after a light lunch on the 18th of December. The procedure was booked for the 19th of December, at about four p.m. I told her that if my sugar level started getting high, I would most definitely be injecting one or two units into my body, depending on what the sugar reading was. I would try and keep the sugar level under 10, and if it started getting too low, I would sip on clear apple juice to bring it up again. She insisted I could not have any insulin at all, but I insisted I would take some if I needed to.

While we were reading through the forms, she got all the dates mixed up that were important guidelines that showed me when to start and finish taking the medication that would clean my bowels out before I was to have the procedure. In my opinion, she was so focused on the fact that I was a diabetic with high blood sugar readings at the time that she wasn't concentrating on the actual procedure date and the dates that I had to start taking the medication to clean my bowels out. Instead of working from the 15th of December towards the 19th of December, she worked backwards and had the procedure date written down as the 11th of December.

She focused so much on the fact that I was a diabetic that I eventually pointed to the model that was on her desk with the colon exposed. I told her the poor model was feeling extremely neglected because he had been standing there for ages and was meant to be the centre of attraction, considering the fact that the topic of discussion was meant to be the colon and not diabetes! It's amazing how it doesn't matter what your reason is for seeing some doctors and nurses; they always seem to be more focused on the diabetes.

I felt very frustrated when I left her room. Remember to keep in mind that this book is all about me, so if I voice my opinion on something or someone, then that is only how I feel about the situation or the person. These are the results of circumstances I have found myself in, and I sometimes wonder if there are any diabetics who feel the same way.

The 19th of December finally arrived, and before I was taken into the theatre, the anaesthetist approached me and asked me what my sugar reading was and if I had taken any insulin whilst I was in the waiting room. I told him that I had tested my blood about half an hour prior to him asking me and that the sugar level was 6, which was pretty good. Before that reading though, it was 9, so I injected one unit into my body. He nodded and said he would have done the same thing. Just for the record: they found a polyp in my colon, removed it, and sent it away for analysis, and I am very happy to say that they did not find any cancer present. You can imagine how much relief that brought to both my family and me.

ANOTHER EPISODE OF 'ARE YOU KIDDING ME!'

I noticed one day that the thumb on my left hand was starting to hurt quite severely. I started off by rubbing it, as anyone would do. The pain had got worse by the next day, so I eventually decided to call the doctor to have it seen. My personal doctor was away on holiday, so I had to make an appointment to see another one. I walked into his room and sat down. He then started asking me several questions about my health. As soon as he learnt I was a diabetic, it was all he wanted to talk about. He wanted to know how much insulin I was taking on a daily basis and what types of insulin I was using. How long I had been a diabetic for and if any other members of my family were diabetics. How often I checked my blood sugar levels and what my readings were. How much long-lasting insulin I was taking and why I was only taking it at night instead of in the morning as well. Did I have any problems with any parts of my body as a result of being a diabetic? In the meantime, my poor, darling little thumb was being completely ignored.

I ended up asking him if he was interested to know why I was actually seeing him. He told me he would get to that part soon. I then told him that I was tired of him talking about my diabetes and that I was there for the sake of my thumb and not my blood! 'Oh, okay,' he said. 'What is wrong with your thumb?' He came to the conclusion that I had probably strained it. I walked out of his room, feeling nothing but annoyed and completely unimpressed. I felt as though I had spent a lot of wasted time talking about something that had nothing to do with the reason I was there.

WHAT I HAVE LEARNT

Facts about Diabetes

- There are so many people who are unaware of the fact that they are diabetics.

- In some cases, there are no symptoms of **Type 2** diabetes in people.

- Diabetes is the main cause of blindness in working-age adults.

- People who have diabetes are twice more likely to develop heart disease than someone who does not have diabetes.

- Diabetes costs $174 billion annually, which includes $116 billion in direct medical expenses.

CHAPTER 10

HOW YOU CAN HELP OTHERS FROM YOUR OWN EXPERIENCES

I was in the grocery store one afternoon, doing my normal weekly shopping, when I suddenly felt a sugar low coming on. I started feeling lethargic, and this was followed by the awful numb feeling in my head. I immediately reached into my handbag and took out a juice box. A man walked up to me and asked me if I was all right. He said he noticed I was looking a bit pale in the face. It looked as if I was very concerned about something too, and he noticed the urgency I projected into getting my hands on the juice box that was in my handbag. He then asked me outright if I was a diabetic.

When I answered his question with 'Yes, I am', he told me about his little girl who was also a diabetic and who was in the hospital with acute nausea and vomiting. He said he and his wife were extremely concerned because this incident had happened a few times before. It was something they were very familiar with, but they did not know what the cause of the problem was. It was very sad that her parents did not know about **ketoacidosis**; the reason I am able to say that is that I asked him, and he replied that he had never heard of that term before. I immediately compared his daughter's symptoms to mine and mentioned the fact that we had no knowledge of **ketoacidosis** in the early years either.

That was my chance to do something really special for a stranger, his wife, and his little girl. It was a chance for me to share one or two of my experiences with him in regard to **ketoacidosis** and, hopefully, to help that family. This incident is one of the reasons I am writing this book. I feel there must be a lot of people who probably feel alone in their struggle with diabetes. Some people may not want to talk about it to others, as they might feel too embarrassed, even though there is no need to feel embarrassed at all. Others might not want to be a burden to anyone, even though that wouldn't be the case.

I must say that it was thrilling knowing that what I was telling this man was very meaningful to him. I said a lot but tried to sum it up as best as I could so that I could make a quick, sharp impression on his mind that would leave him feeling confident that there was hope their daughter would conquer the repetitive act of having to feel so terribly ill and end up in the hospital for weeks at a time. I know you are probably wondering what the miracle cure is that I am referring to. Well, it's the one source nobody can survive without—water! It is that amazing liquid we are all so dependent on to keep us alive. We would not be able to survive without it. So it makes a lot of sense then that if we are suffering from dehydration, after a while we will no doubt end up in the hospital. Being a diabetic for more than twenty-five years and experimenting along the way, I found that good old water is the best thing for me to bring my ketones down, as long as I catch it before it gets out of hand. By that, I mean that as soon as I start to feel dehydrated and I feel nausea setting in, I immediately check my ketones, and I start drinking bottles of water. I have, on numerous occasions, mentioned the water fact to others, as I have found that it worked for me.

SPORTS AND DIABETES

Along my journey of incidences and with everyday living, I have at times heard some diabetics say that they are not able to participate in sporting activities because of their medical condition. My personal opinion in regard to that is, don't let diabetes hold you back! Unless your doctor has a valid reason you shouldn't participate in sporting activities—for example, if you have an injury of some sort—then I cannot see any reason for you to be sitting on a bench and munching on a burger or whatever you like eating and watching other people exercise while you are not. Again, I am only talking from my own experiences. For me, it's not a disease that limits you from living a normal life. You are the person who limits yourself in every sense of the word. I am obviously a diabetic who presently has not lost any limbs and is not on dialysis; in order for me to keep my body healthy, I will always exercise and should always eat healthy meals, but I must admit that I don't walk the straight and narrow line altogether. There is a bit of cheating along the way when it comes to food, but I do limit myself more often than not.

I have always been involved in sporting activities. I strongly believe that when I ended up in the hospital numerous times, it was nothing but my fitness level that kept me hanging on by a thread. I had nothing to lose by staying fit and enjoying outdoor and even indoor sporting activities. It does three things for you: It keeps you fit, and it takes your mind off the everyday living stresses. In so doing, you work off any negative feelings that might be burdening you. It also keeps you looking fabulous.

In saying this, being a diabetic is always quite traumatising, either when you first discover you are one or, if you allow it to, when you become permanently depressed. Therefore, I personally vote for participating in at least one sport! I am fifty-seven years old, and when I was younger, I used to think that anybody who was at the age of fifty might as well start digging their own grave. I used to think they were ancient! But now that the ripe old age of fifty has come and gone, I still feel exactly the same way as I did when I was in my twenties, with one small difference—that my body lets me know I'm not twenty years old anymore. Does that mean it's time to sit down in an armchair and wait to die? Absolutely not! It could be that way if I allowed it to happen. On some days, I have absolutely no energy and even have pain in my feet and legs, but I get out of bed and make myself carry on with everyday living. The best thing for me is to saddle up my horse, whose name is Bobby, and go for a ride. I guarantee you that after a ride, whatever pain and lethargic feeling I had before will have left me once the ride is over.

On other occasions, I'll get on my bicycle and go for a ride, and once again, I will come home, feeling as if I'm on top of the world. My friend Wendy and I love going on bicycle rides together. It's always a great idea to have someone to do a sporting activity with. You guys should give it a go too. Another alternative is to get on my scooter and go for a ride down the road and come home feeling great. Taking the dogs to the beach and even on a walk around the block is another way to get some exercise. I also enjoy using the treadmill, and one of the most effortless exercises I do is using the vibration platform.

About a year ago, I had a friend who also loved going on beach walks with me, and we used to take my dogs with us. We used to do night walks to avoid being sunburnt. I always made sure I had a supply of jelly beans or two juice boxes with me, just in case I have a sugar low. We used to walk for ages, and after the walk, we would buy something to eat and drink. So, you see, you can live a normal life. You just have to be prepared at all times for any situation that may arise. I have a saying that I live by: 'Don't try and fight against diabetes. You won't win the battle. Try and work with it instead!' By that, I mean when it shakes you up. For example, when you have a sugar low, feed it sugar. When there is too much sugar in your system, feed it insulin. When you are feeling miserable and depressed, take yourself out for a walk or do some form of sport or, if you don't feel like doing exercises on that particular day, phone a friend and invite them over for a cup of tea and have a chat, instead of allowing your illness to chew you up and get the better of you.

There's something to be depressed about, but I have managed to overcome it by making another plan. I am a great tennis fan! I have always loved the game, and my friend Colleen and I used to play every week, on Tuesday afternoons. Did I have problems on the court with my diabetes? Yes, on the odd occasion, I did. I would say I had sugar lows about three times in one year. Not bad at all.

Before we started playing tennis together, I let her know I was a diabetic, and I told her what to do if I suddenly got a sugar low that I was unable to control. The only reason I've had sugar lows on the tennis court was because I did not listen to the warning signs. Whilst we were in the middle of a game, I got that numb feeling in my head and started to feel weak, but I chose to ignore it and thought that once one of us hits the tennis ball into the net, I would quickly get my hands on a juice box and/or jelly beans. But because I didn't react immediately, I was hit really hard with a low on one particular day.

All my friends have learnt to be aware of my symptoms. Before I actually stopped playing, she asked me if I was feeling okay. She said I had that look on my face that told her I was having a low. I sat down on the court, and she handed me a juice box. Luckily, I had educated her about my condition and had also told her that I had the juice boxes and jelly beans in my bag. I drank the juice, and after a while, I was able to carry on with the game. I'm very sad to say that we no longer play tennis together because of a torn calf muscle that now only limits me to certain sporting activities.

Another incident I would like to mention is when my daughter, Carrin, and I went to our first yoga class together. I had never done yoga in my life before, and I must say that it was a good workout without high-impact exercise. I'm sure there must be millions of you out there who attend yoga classes. Anyway, there we were, stretching to our hearts' content with the other girls in the class, and I could not believe how much of a sweat we had all built up. It must have been about twenty minutes into the exercise when Carrin, who was on a mat beside me, asked me if I was feeling okay. She then asked me if I was having a low. I wasn't quite sure up until that point, so I told her I would let her know in a short while.

But Carrin has been around me and my diabetes for such a long time, and she could tell I was about to find myself in a lot of trouble if she didn't do something about it straight away. She got up during the class and fetched me a juice box. The yoga instructor was aware of my condition and kept her eyes on me during the lesson. Unfortunately, one juice box just wasn't enough. Carrin noticed it again, so she got up off the floor and fetched a second juice box for me to drink. Well, that didn't seem to be helping either, so she went to her car and brought me a sweet to eat. Within seconds, I was feeling good again. I can't stress enough how important it is for you to let people know about your condition, as I always do. It just seems to come in handy all the time. On that night though, for some or other reason, I didn't feel the low coming on. I found that to be rather strange.

Unfortunately for me, I have torn my right calf muscle four times in total. The first tear happened two years ago whilst I was riding my scooter, and the other three happened last year. The second one happened one very cold morning, after I had woken up and went downstairs into the garden and leapt forward to run. The third one happened when I fell off my horse, and the fourth one happened when I was exercising on the treadmill. I was obviously unable to walk properly, and for one whole year, I was not able to do any form of sports. I think that during that year, I had the worst time ever as far as my diabetes was concerned. Because I was unable to do any form of exercise, I did the next best thing. I had an excuse to overeat! Eating and watching TV seem to go hand in hand very well. That was not a good choice to make. Of course, the shape of my body started changing too. I was turning into a little round ball and was feeling very uncomfortable with myself.

I have learnt something over the years that I never used to be aware of, and that is that whenever I ate something that was a naughty food, **BAM** – CFS!!!!! I would inject too much insulin into my body to try and keep the sugar level down, and because of that, I would end up having a low. Then I would have to eat or drink something sugary to bring the sugar level back up again, but when I checked my reading, the sugar level would once again be too high. So I would inject more insulin into my body. This used to be extremely frustrating, and it was an awful roller-coaster ride. I could never seem to reach a good reading and keep it stable. I can't help but wonder how many people are out there right now, suffering from the very same thing.

I used to drag myself to the back door and call my horse. He would come over for a treat of carrots, which took me forever to give him, because I would have to go down the steps at a snail's pace, and then the trip back up took even longer. A blood clot had also formed in my calf muscle, so I was on blood thinners. So there I was—a diabetic who was getting bigger and bigger in size, hobbling along on crutches because my calf muscle was torn, dependent on blood thinners to protect my lungs, heart, and brain against clots which, of course, could have put me six feet under and could have had me pushing up daisies! I was eating all the wrong foods but enjoyed every single bite. **BAM** – CFS!!!!! So, you see, we are all guilty at times, when given the opportunity to be naughty.

Anyway, after a year, when it was safe for me to carry on with my sporting activities as normal, I started getting the zest for life again. I'm disappointed to say that I don't play squash anymore either, but I do play table tennis instead; also, I do still ride my horse and bicycle, swim, and go for walks. So, you see, a completely different reason has prevented me from doing two of my favourite sporting activities. Having diabetes cannot always be blamed for everything.

WHAT I HAVE LEARNT

How can diabetes affect the eyes?

High blood glucose and high blood pressure causes small blood vessels to swell, and they leak liquid into the retina of the eye. This blurs the vision and can sometimes lead to blindness. People who have diabetes are also more likely to develop cataracts and glaucoma. Cataracts are clouding of the eye's lens, and glaucoma is damage of the optic nerve. A person can undergo laser surgery to help these conditions. You can prevent eye problems though. By keeping your blood glucose level close to normal, you can prevent or delay the onset of diabetic eye disease. Keeping your blood pressure under control is also important. Finding and treating eye problems early can help save sight.

Regular eye examinations are highly recommended, because if there are any problems with your eyes, they can already be noticed in the early stages.

CHAPTER 11

SOME SCARY MOMENTS MANY YEARS AGO

THE FIRST ONE

I am presently using two types of insulin. The first one is short-acting insulin, and the second one is long-acting insulin. I have been using these insulins for a period of approximately twelve years.

A few years ago, I was on a dosage of long-acting insulin twice daily. I took a dose in the morning and at night before I went to bed. I was taking fifteen units in the morning and fifteen units at night. Along with that dosage, I was taking the short-acting insulin throughout the day, and the amounts I was injecting into my body depended on the amount of food and what I was eating, which meant I was on a sliding scale. Every day at 3 p.m., I would end up having a low. I used to dread that time of the day, because I knew I was going to take a nosedive into that dreaded sugar low. I always had the jelly beans and juice boxes ready, but I still had to go through that awful feeling of having my sugar level dropping too low and then having to put up with that terrible lethargic feeling as well.

Then one fine day, friends of ours who lived in a different town from us contacted us to let us know they were going to come for a visit and spend a weekend with us. We were very pleased to hear the good news, but little did I know that I was about to learn something that would make my every afternoon a lot easier from then onwards.

They arrived the following weekend, and my friend's daughter just happened to be a diabetic as well. That came in very handy, because Sherry and I were able to discuss diabetes and fully understand each other's needs, discomforts, anxieties, and exciting moments. She was very clued-up on the disease, with having to take care of her daughter.

On Saturday afternoon, we decided to take a drive to the beach and go for a long lovely walk along the sand. We spoke about so many different events that had occurred with her daughter and me. I had my eye on the clock, and sure as nuts, as three o'clock was approaching, I started getting all the symptoms of a sugar low. I told her I needed to drink a juice box before I felt good enough to carry on with the walk.

She pointed out something to me. She wondered why I was taking a large dose of long-acting insulin in the morning as well as at night. She suggested that I try cutting out the long-acting insulin in the morning. She told me she only gave her daughter long-acting insulin at night, at bedtime. She thought that maybe if I did that, those awful lows might stop happening. It was well worth the try, and I immediately adopted that way of living. That was pretty much the last time I had regular lows in the afternoons. It made my life so much easier! Have I had anymore lows since that day? Yes, I have, but not necessarily at the same time each day anymore.

THE SECOND ONE

Many years ago, when I was driving my car home from town, I was hit by a sugar low. I wasn't too far away from my house, and I just hoped I would be able to get home in time to eat or drink something that was sugary. But as always happens, there is a warning, and if it is not taken care of immediately, the drop in your sugar level gets the better of you. I was in a very bad way, knowing that I did not have anything that contained sugar in my car to pick me up again. That was a rare thing to happen to me. I always make sure I carry something sweet on hand in case of an emergency.

I was driving up a street and was looking for the street which was the turn-off to our house. The street that would have taken me home was directly opposite the high school, so you really couldn't miss it. But my sugar level had got so low that I ended up not seeing the street or even the school. As I drove, I thankfully noticed the bakery I had seen so many times before. I parked my car on the side of the road and walked in. The lady at the counter was serving a little boy who had bought a piece of cake, but knowing I had no time to waste, I opened the door of one of the cold drink fridges, grabbed a bottle of soft drink, opened it, and started pouring it down my throat. Well, the poor shopkeeper went into a fit of panic and reminded me that I had to pay for the drink before I consumed it. I literally ignored her and kept on drinking, but then a thought crept into my mind. What if she calls the police, and I end up spending time in jail? After all, the lady had no idea who I was or why I was drinking her cold drink before paying for it.

Anyway, I eventually stopped sucking on the bottle and told her I was in desperate need of the drink, but I assured her I was not going to do a runner trick on her and disappear with her bottle of soft drink. The poor darling was relieved, and I was finally able to hand the money to her over the counter. I got into my car and drove home. You should never go anywhere without having something sweet on hand to prevent you from possibly passing out.

THE THIRD ONE

One day, while I was spending my time at home, I could feel my three o'clock visitor moving in—the dreaded low! Anyway, that was another one of those times when I didn't respond to it immediately and only decided to do something about the situation once it was already too far gone. I wanted to check my blood sugar reading even though it was obvious what was happening to me; as all diabetics will know, when your sugar level goes down to that degree, you can get beyond reasoning.

While I was squeezing my finger for the blood to come out, my daughter walked into the house through the front door and asked me what I was doing. When I told her that I wanted to do a blood test but that the blood would not come out, she took hold of my finger and did the blood test for me. The reading was 2.1. She told me there was so much blood, but I was unable to see it. Carrin had just come home from school, and when she walked into the house and saw me, she told me I looked like someone who was on drugs or was very drunk. I've often wondered if anyone else has ever thought that of me.

THE FOURTH ONE

One night, after having cooked dinner and tidied up the kitchen, I decided to relax on the couch in the lounge and watch TV. I remember being quite naughty with the pudding after having dinner (**BAM – CFS!!!!!**) and giving myself a high dose of insulin to counteract the high sugar reading that would have occurred. Charl was away at work that night, and both our children were out with their friends. As I sat there, I suddenly felt very strange. As soon as I started sweating, I realised what was happening to me. I was having a sugar low. My sugar level had gone down too far by then, so I was unable to reason.

I looked at one of the sockets in the wall, and I was trying to figure out if I was meant to put my finger into one of the holes so that I could feel better. I also tried to work out if I needed insulin or not. At that point, I told myself I was in trouble, and then I thought I might need to make my way to the kitchen, where the fridge was. I stumbled down the passage like a drunken person, running into the walls. When I got to the kitchen, I made my way over to the fridge and opened the fridge door. I opened it and stared at all the contents but could not make head or tail of what they all were. I was looking at milk, soft drinks, salads, cheese, and so much more, but none of those items made any sense to me. I was trying to work out what everything was.

In the meantime, the clock was ticking, and I was getting to the stage where I thought I was going to pass out. In desperation, I bent down and just took something from the inside of the fridge door and put it in my mouth. I then realised it was a can. It was as if I was going through stages of being unaware and then aware of what was going on, and I started drinking from the open can of soft drink.

While this was all going on, I kept on talking to myself, because I knew I was in serious trouble. But after I started drinking the soft drink, I could feel myself getting back to normal again. My body went into complete shock. When I was able to reason properly again, I saw myself in the bathroom mirror. I was so pale and was saturated with sweat. I had a shower immediately after that and then went back to the couch and just sat there, trying to take in what had just happened.

THE FIFTH ONE

On another occasion, after Charl, the kids, and I had gone to bed, Charl woke me up at 11 p.m. He said he woke up from a deep sleep to find that the bed was sopping wet. When he turned the light on to find out what the cause was or where it was coming from, he realised it was coming from me. I was saturated in sweat. I was having a sugar low. He rushed to the kitchen and took a slice of chocolate cake out of the fridge. He then woke me up and told me to eat the cake.

I remember sitting up in the bed and staring at him, with no understanding of what was going on. He brought the cake towards my mouth and told me to start eating. I then passed out, and fell backwards on to the bed. Fortunately, I regained consciousness almost immediately, and the next thing I knew, there were two paramedics in the bedroom. They asked me if I was able to orally have glucose. I nodded, and one of the paramedics squirted some of it into my mouth. It helped me a great deal, and I very quickly started coming out of the low and feeling good again.

They wanted to take me to the hospital for observation, but I knew I didn't need to go with them. I then thanked Charl and them for taking care of me, and then the paramedics got back into the ambulance and left. I then had a shower, changed my nightclothes and the bedding, and had a coffee with Charl, and then we climbed back into bed and went to sleep. Before we climbed back into bed, however, we had a long discussion about what had just happened. I obviously had taken too much insulin to counteract the amount of carbs and sugar I had eaten at dinner time.

THE SIXTH ONE

One day, I met up with a friend at the shopping mall for breakfast. She is one of my dearest friends, who lives about 25 kilometres away from where we live. It's always fun catching up with her. She is one of those people who I don't have to see or hear from every day, but when we catch up with one another, it's as if we haven't missed a moment without seeing each other. It is a very special friendship!

We met at the food court, where we sat down to a lovely meal and lots of chit-chat. After about two hours, we were ready to leave the food court and do some clothes shopping. There's nothing like having a girls' day out. We walked into a number of clothing stores, but when we walked into one store in particular, we were very interested in their line of clothing. We shuffled through the kids', men's, and women's clothing sections, and we had a great time looking at the DVDs, books, sweets and chocolates, kitchenware, and just about every department of the store. I don't normally go shopping with friends, so this was a different experience. It was so much fun.

We were in the store for quite a long time when I started feeling lethargic. I never told her how I was feeling, but because she knew me so well, she asked me if I was feeling okay. I just shook my head, and she took me by the arm and led me to the only bench that was in the store and told me to sit down. She also told me to check my blood. The reading was 2.5. I had two juice boxes in my handbag. I took one out, and she opened it for me to drink. It didn't seem to be helping, so she took out the second one and gave that to me to drink too. After a while, I felt good enough to walk again, and we were on our way out of the store. We felt that we had had a wonderful day together but that it was time to go home.

THE SEVENTH ONE

One Friday afternoon, Charl and I decided to have a rest, and so off to bed we went. He woke up some time before I did, but when I woke up, I was covered in sweat. I was having a low! My sugar had dropped so low that I was unable to call Charl for help. As hard as I tried, I just couldn't seem to get my vocal chords to do their job properly.

Charl, at the time, was downstairs and under the house (we live in a high-set house), and he was busy doing mechanical work on the ride-on mower. He needed to come upstairs for a drink of cold water, which was an absolute blessing. When he came into the house, I tried to call him again. He heard a noise coming from our bedroom, but he wasn't sure if it was coming from me or something else. When he walked into the room, I saw the shocked look on his face. He could very clearly see that I was in serious trouble. I was having another low!

Because he had seen this so many times before, he knew exactly how to react to help get me out of the situation I was in. He went to the kitchen and came back with a juice box for me to drink. As I drank it, it felt as if my sugar level was dropping even more. He asked me if I was feeling any better, and all I could do was shake my head to indicate that I wasn't feeling better at all. He then went back to the kitchen and came back with a glass of soft drink. He gave it to me, and I started drinking that too. I still could not feel any improvement, and then I managed to whisper to him that I needed a sweet that was kept in the pantry. As soon as I started eating it, I could feel the change taking place. It was working, and my sugar level was picking up again.

After having taken in so much sugar, I had to then keep on checking my blood sugar readings, because it was obvious my sugar level was going to go in the opposite direction. I went through the night, checking my blood sugar readings at hourly intervals. By the following morning, I was completely exhausted and was so sick of having this disease.

THE EIGHTH ONE

My daughter, Carrin, has lived with me as a diabetic all her life, as has my son, CJ. Carrin has pretty much fine-tuned me as a diabetic. She is able to pinpoint exactly when I am in the process of getting a low.

She was driving my car one day, with me sitting in the passenger seat next to her. We were having a general discussion, when she suddenly asked me if I was feeling all right. She noticed I was slurring my words, and I also knew I was heading for another low. I was and am always very aware of having some form of sugar on me, but again, on that day, I had nothing left in my handbag that I could eat or drink to bring my sugar level up. Carrin drove to the shopping mall and told me to stay in the car while she ran into the pharmacy. It only felt like seconds, and she returned with a packet of jelly beans. She opened the packet and told me to start eating.

I love the taste of jelly beans, but I really can't stand the taste of the purple ones. Carrin, on the other hand, loves them. I put my hand into the packet and took out a purple jelly bean and offered it to her. The poor girl was getting quite worried because I was more concerned about her not eating her purple jelly bean than I was about eating mine. She put the jelly bean into her mouth and started chewing, and then I was quite happy to eat my few.

Carrin told me, once everything had settled down and was back to normal, that when she walked into the pharmacy, there were a lot of people waiting in the queue to be served; but she walked past all of them and told one of the ladies who was busy serving a customer that I was in the car outside and that she urgently needed to get the jelly beans in me. So the lady served Carrin before she even finished serving the customer she was busy with at the time. It's good to know there are people out there who understand and listen to the importance of a medical emergency when it is needed.

At this stage, I think I should summarise a list of the symptoms I have felt over the years. I have since learned how to listen to my body and respond more quickly now than I used to in the earlier stages.

- I would start sweating a lot, so it looked as if I had been swimming with my clothes on.

- I would feel dizzy.

- I would feel lethargic and feel the need to sit or lie down.

- I would get slurred speech and sound like a drunken person.

- I couldn't reason. I never had a clue where I was, and I couldn't figure out what I was supposed to do to help myself get out of the situation. I found that I would try to work out if I should have been taking insulin or not. That only happened when I ignored the warning signs.

- I would get very sleepy and could fall asleep almost immediately.

- I'd look at a book or a magazine, and I wouldn't be able to read the words that were written down.

WHAT I HAVE LEARNT

Diabetes and Colds or Flu?

Being ill can raise your blood glucose level. Very often, when you are ill, it prevents you from eating properly, which also affects the blood glucose level.

Diabetes can make the immune system more vulnerable to severe cases of the flu. People with diabetes who come down with the flu may get very sick and may even have to go to the hospital. It is a good idea to have a flu shot once a year to lessen your chances of getting ill.

What to Do When I Am Sick

Keep on taking your diabetes pills or insulin. Don't stop taking them even if you can't eat.

Test your blood glucose every four hours and keep track of the results.

Drink extra (calorie-free) liquids and try to eat as you normally would. If you can't, try to have soft foods and liquids containing the equivalent amount of carbohydrates that you usually consume.

Weigh yourself every day. Losing weight without trying is a sign of high blood glucose.

Call your healthcare provider or go to an emergency room if any of the following happen to you:

- You feel too sick to eat normally and are unable to keep down food for more than six hours.

- You're having severe diarrhoea.

- You lose 5 pounds or more.

- Your temperature is over 101 degrees Fahrenheit.

- Your blood glucose is lower than 60 milligrams per decilitre or remains over 300 milligrams per decilitre.

- You have moderate or large amounts of ketones in your urine.

- You're having trouble breathing.

- You feel sleepy or can't think clearly.

CHAPTER 12

PEOPLE'S OPINIONS OF ME AS A DIABETIC

I can't help but wonder how many of you out there have sometimes felt a bit annoyed at your friends and family members. These are the people who do not know what it is like to be walking in your shoes yet seem to think they know more than you do about the disease. I don't mind that people ask me questions all the time about diabetes, because I like to think I am teaching them something about the subject. But when I answer their questions and they reply with 'Are you sure?' it really frustrates me.

A perfect example is when I was having lunch with a crowd of girls one day, and I told them I didn't want to eat any extra food because that would mean I would need to have another insulin injection. One of the girls asked me if I was sure I would need to do that. This came from someone who was not a diabetic, yet she had doubts about what I was saying. When I asked her if she knew anything about the disease, she said she didn't. When I asked her why she second-guessed me, she told me that she wasn't sure but that it just didn't sound right.

On another occasion, I was told by an ex-friend that she wondered if my diabetes was the cause of my lashing out at her at times. Sometimes people will use the disease as an excuse against you, but at the end of the day, that is just their opinion. I do know that diabetes can affect a person's mood, but so can hormones, a headache, a bad hair day, or anything else.

Many a time, when I have broken out in a sweat because my sugar level has gone too low, people have asked me if I needed insulin. 'No thank you! Do you want to kill me? I need sugar!' That is just due to a lack of knowledge on their part. It's okay though, not everyone can be expected to know about diabetes, and in some cases like these, those people are at least trying to be helpful.

On many occasions, some people will treat you with the utmost care if they know about your condition. I have friends, and definitely all my family members, who are fine-tuned to my diabetes. For example, when I am out having dinner with them, you can rest assured that someone at the table will ask me if I've taken my insulin. It goes to show how much the special people in your life really do care about you. Very often, when I meet up with a friend or a family member, the same question arises: 'How is it going with your diabetes?' For me, that is awesome. Hearing the same question over and over again can be a bit daunting, but they truly want to know that I am taking good care of myself.

One night, we attended a birthday celebration dinner. One of the men who was there turned out to be very interested in the topic of diabetes. He started a discussion with me, and one thing led to the next. At first, the conversation was going well, but as the night progressed, he started becoming very personal and knocking my character down based on the fact that I was a diabetic.

At first, I didn't want to cause a scene, so I chose to be the better person and took his comments with a pinch of salt. But after a long while, I could not restrain myself anymore. I let him know what I was thinking, and then all that unnecessary friction came to an end. He was incredibly sarcastic and told me he realised that when I was grumpy towards him, it was due to diabetes. Oh, nonsense! I have learnt to ignore the comments from people who have used diabetes against me, and life is so much easier now. I'm not sure if any of you have felt the same way.

On another occasion, a group of us, friends and family, went to a restaurant for lunch. The restaurant was packed with people. It had a lovely atmosphere about it, and it was one of our favourite lunch and dinner catch-up places. After standing in a queue for a long time, we were escorted to our dinner table. In that restaurant, you order your food at the entrance, and then it gets brought over to your table.

After we had all started the evening with drinks and chats around the table, I decided to go to the ladies' restroom so that I could take a dose of insulin before our meals arrived. When I walked into the restroom, one of the toilets was occupied, and the other one was vacant. There was a lady standing at the hand-wash basin, and she was facing the vacant toilet. I asked her if she was going to use the toilet, as I didn't want to seem as if I was being rude by pushing in. She told me she did not need to use it, so I went in.

While I was in there, I took my insulin pen out of my handbag and used it. It only took a few minutes to do, and then I opened the toilet door and walked out. The lady was still standing at the hand-wash basin, and I smiled at her and walked past her. There was a look of utmost disgust on her face. All I could think of was that she must have thought I was very unhygienic because I did not wash my hands or flush after using the toilet. I looked at her, smiled, and said, 'I didn't need to use the toilet. I only needed to go in there to shoot up.' Well, the look on her face after I said that was one of shock. I then made my way back to our dinner table. Shortly after that, our meals were brought over to us, and we all started munching away.

It was such a lovely, light-hearted night. Then somewhere in the middle of it all, I happened to look up, and I saw the lady who had been in the toilet, looking at me, together with a number of other people too. Her dinner table was to the left of ours. I could see the look on everyone's faces. I could imagine them saying to one another, 'That lady uses drugs!' With that happening, I told everyone at our table what had happened and what was happening as a result, and everyone thought that that was hilarious! If I had worded my sentence differently and explained to her that I was a diabetic, the situation would have been completely different. I was definitely a topic of discussion at their table that night.

I have nothing against people who use drugs. Everyone has their own reasons and preferences that they do different things, but the fact that the people at that table could not keep their eyes off me made me sensitive to what I thought they were thinking.

WHAT I HAVE LEARNT

It is very important to take care of my feet if I have diabetes!

Nerve damage, circulation problems, and infections can cause serious foot problems for people with diabetes. Nerve damage can sometimes be the result of deformed or misshapen feet, and that causes pressure points that can turn into blisters, sores, or ulcers. With poor circulation, these injuries can take very long to heal. Sometimes this can lead to amputation of a toe, foot, or leg.

Caring for Your Feet

- Cuts, cracks, sores, red spots, swelling, infected toenails, splinters, blisters, and calluses on the feet that do not heal after one day are all reasons you should call on your doctor to have them seen.

- Wash your feet in warm water and be sure to dry them well.

- Rub lotion on the tops and bottoms of your feet. It is not advised to rub lotion between your toes. This avoids cracking and drying.

- Wear stockings or socks when wearing your shoes. This should prevent your feet from forming blisters.

- Always protect your feet by wearing shoes or slippers so that you don't stand on anything that will pierce your feet, such as nails, splinters, etc.

- Your feet should never be exposed to too much heat or cold.

- When sitting, keep the blood flowing to your lower limbs by propping your feet up and moving your toes and ankles for a few minutes at a time.

- Smoking prevents blood flow to the feet, so it is a good idea to try and avoid it.

- Keep your blood sugar, blood pressure, and cholesterol under control by eating healthy foods, staying active, and taking your diabetes medicines.

CHAPTER 13

THESE ARE THE THINGS THAT I KEEP IN MIND EVERYDAY

- Every morning when I wake up, I have a notepad ready so that I can keep track of how well I perform my diabetic schedule during the course of the day. If you are under the care and supervision of a diabetic educator, he or she will normally issue you with a diary for this purpose. Below is an example of how I do it.

Date	Time	Finger	Reading	Insulin	Meal
11/11	12.10	R1	10.2	3NR	Cheese and biscuits

- If my reading is too high—for example, above 4.5—I will give myself one unit of short-acting insulin for every 3 points that need to be lessened, so one unit of short-acting insulin = 3 points. If my sugar reading is 10 and it should be 4.5, I should give myself two units of insulin. I do believe, however, that our bodies all work slightly differently at times. For me, I would have only taken one unit of short-acting insulin, because two units would have put me on a low. I've had to experiment with my body over the past few years.

- I've noticed that whenever I eat according to the carbohydrate count on packages of different foods, the amount of insulin I should be injecting into my body doesn't always keep my sugar reading on track. I sometimes find that I have to give myself a bigger dose of insulin. This is how my body responds to the suggested dosages.

- I have noticed that if I inject insulin into my body in the morning and then am active without eating something first, my sugar level goes sky-high. Even if I am not hungry, I will always eat something before I start my day, and the same applies to doing any form of exercise. I will always eat something before using the treadmill, riding my horse, or even just going on a long walk.

- I always check that I have enough insulin in my handbag before leaving to go shopping or to a restaurant. I have, on more than one occasion, ordered a meal and opened my handbag to get the insulin out, only to discover that my insulin pen only had one or two units left in it. That completely spoils your meal and, in fact, your whole day or night, depending on when you plan to go home. I've had to ask the waitress to pack my meal in a takeaway container so that I could at least eat the meal that I ordered—and paid for—at home.

- I have one thing that I do at night before I go to bed. I look at my diary of all the food I have eaten during the day, and then on the same page, I draw a circle which resembles a dinner plate. As I read down the page, I draw every single piece of food on the plate. That way, I can see exactly how much food and what the food was that I had eaten on that day. For me, it's a mind game. It helps me slow down on my food intake, because if the plate looks too full, I feel annoyed at myself, which is not what I want. But if the plate isn't too full, I feel thrilled with achievement. This is also a way to keep my weight under control.

- It is very important to let the people in your life know you are a diabetic! You could be at work, at the gym, or even just hanging out with friends, and have a sugar low; and if people are not aware of what is going on with you when you start feeling faint and start to sweat and slur your words, they won't know how to help you get out of the situation you are in. If you do end up passing out and somebody calls an ambulance, that person can at least inform the hospital that you are a diabetic, which will enable the paramedics to know exactly what they are dealing with before they reach you.

- I always keep myself hydrated. I check my ketones at least twice a week to see if I am suffering from the beginning stages of **ketoacidosis**, before I reach the stage of having to go to the hospital.

- I have learnt along the way that when something or someone stresses me out, my sugar readings always go sky-high. We all stress about the things that go wrong in life, and that is normal. But it was important for me to learn how not to let the petty things in life affect me anymore. Before I did that, my blood sugar readings were always double figures, but now that I have made those changes, my stress levels have decreased considerably. My blood sugar readings are so much better now.

- Diabetes used to leave me feeling frustrated, because I got so tired of having to prick my fingers all the time, wondering if or when I would get the next sugar low, being labelled by whoever I came in contact with, and so many other reasons. But I have now accepted the fact that I can't fight against the disease. I can only work with it. I have learnt to love myself again and not envy the people who are not diabetics. I no longer feel the need to have to explain myself to others. I am who I am, and what I have, I know how to deal with. I have so much to be thankful for, and I focus on all those things now.

- Sometimes people wonder how many times a day they should check their sugar readings. I check mine at least six times a day. Everyone is different, so you might want to check yours more or less than six times a day. We all work out the things that work best for us as individuals. I used to have a friend who only checked his reading one day a week. I used to tell him that that wasn't nearly enough, but he still kept on doing that. It wasn't a clever move, in my opinion. He unfortunately passed away two years ago.

- We all know that saying 'Life is short', and it really is. So I live my life to the full! I play sports, go shopping, go out to dinners, and do all the things life has to offer. There is no need to make excuses not to do the things other people do to enjoy life, unless you are instructed by your doctor.

- Most important of all is to remember that eating the diabetic way is a healthy way to eat. If everyone ate like we do, people would be a lot healthier, in my opinion. We can allow ourselves treats. There are so many healthy recipes and sugar-free sweets that are available to us.

- I always think of my body parts as individuals. My eyes, kidneys, liver, limbs—all rely on me for their well-being. With every wrong sweet treat or fatty meal and high-carb food that you eat, your organs will suffer. This is just my way of remembering to take care of myself.

- It is very important for me to moisturise my feet and legs every night before going to bed, because if I don't, I will feel pain all night long. Rubbing the moisturiser into my feet and legs seems to help with the circulation, which enables me to have a peaceful sleep.

- If I eat anything that increases the sugar level in my body, I can immediately feel the result in my eyes. They get watery. I personally think that going blind must be one of the most terrifying experiences, and I hope and pray that it never happens to me.

WHAT I HAVE LEARNT

One of the causes of **Type 1** diabetes may be related to cold weather and as is more often develops in winter than in summer. It is more prevalent in places with cold climates.

People who have got low levels of vitamin D are more prone to **Type 2** diabetes. Vitamin D is synthesized from sunlight. People who are not exposed to enough sunshine who lives in the more northerly latitudes are at a higher risk of developing diabetes.

CHAPTER 14

BEDTIME STORY

Well, I have almost come to the end of my life story as a diabetic. There is, however, one very personal subject that has not been discussed, and that is lovemaking.

Don't worry, this is not going to be an erotic storytelling session.

As Mother Nature has it, we all have our needs. Even diabetics have the same needs. In the very beginning, diabetes used to interfere with my husband's and my love life. You know how it goes. You get into the mood of things, and off you go to the bedroom or wherever else. One thing led to another, and then before we knew it, I realised my blood sugar level was dropping. That was a very big turn-off for both of us. Oh dear, such a disappointment!

Things have changed a lot for us since then. Before we get into the mood, I always tell my husband I want to check my blood sugar reading first so that we won't be interrupted. If the blood sugar reading is a bit high, at around 7 or 8, I'll leave it be; but if it is very high, around 10 or 14, I will take one or two units of insulin, depending on the reading, to bring it down. If it is low, around 4.5–6, I will have a bit of a sugar treat, which is usually a fruit juice. That way, I am sure we won't be interrupted by an unwanted guest. This works for us.

I feel the need to discuss this point because I can't help but wonder if there are any diabetics out there whose love lives have come to an abrupt halt or who feel afraid of disappointing their partner and therefore choose not to make love. That, in turn, could possibly affect their relationship as a whole.

WHAT I HAVE LEARNT

Because the symptoms are so easily missed, diabetes is known as the silent killer.

In 1980, there were a 108 million cases of diabetics compared to 422 million in 2014. This is a big issue.

Sugar is in almost everything that we eat these days so gone all the days when sugar was only expected to be in certain food.

CHAPTER 15

AN UNEXPECTED CHANGE

As life has it, there is always room for change and surprises. Something unexpectedly happened to me some time ago that had both me and my husband a bit baffled.

As I have already mentioned, the months of April and May are always a very worrying time for me and my family. During the month of April this year, I managed to escape getting ill, and I was hoping I would escape it too during the month of May. Unfortunately, that did not happen.

It was a Friday morning, and we were about two weeks into May. I woke up with the dreaded nausea and violent stomach cramps. I got out of bed and made a cup of tea. After I had finished drinking the tea, I took a bottle of water out of the fridge and started drinking that too. I knew I needed to put a lot of water into my body so that I could start fighting off the ketones. The water had no sooner reached my stomach than I started vomiting. I checked my ketones straight away and saw that I definitely had **ketoacidosis** once again. My ketone reading was 0.6.

Charl looked at me and said, 'Oh no, do we have to take you to the hospital?' I told him to let me try and get the situation under control before we rushed off to the hospital. I drank another huge gulp of water, and up it came again. The vomiting had set in, which normally would make it very obvious that I did actually need to go to the hospital. I told Charl that if I continued to vomit and if it got really bad, I would call an ambulance, as I would obviously not be able to drive myself into town. Charl was about to leave for work. He works away from home for a week at a time, so it was very worrying for him to leave me alone at home whilst this was going on. I promised him I would not ignore the fact that I needed to go to the hospital if it came to that, but I told him that I just felt I could possibly prevent myself from having to. When he left in his car, he phoned our son, CJ, and asked him to keep an eye on me, which he did.

CJ sent me text messages and phoned me throughout the entire day, and I saw a lot of him on the weekend too. He was wonderful. When Charl spoke to him on the phone, he told CJ I needed to get some more ketone strips, as I would be testing my ketones regularly during the day and night. CJ phoned me and asked me to send him a photo of the box of strips that I used, and he went to a drugstore and bought me two boxes. I was so appreciative of both my husband and my son with the way they took care of me.

CJ told me to do a ketone test right there and then, and after I had done that, the reading did not look good at all. It had gone from 0.6 earlier on in the morning to 1.7. It had increased quite considerably, which was extremely worrying. CJ wondered if he should take me to the hospital, but the strange thing was that I noticed an incredible difference in the pattern of it all. I noticed that whenever I drank black tea or coffee, I did not vomit, but as soon as I drank water, I started vomiting straight away. Another thing that was very unusual was that Charl did not notice any fruity odour coming from my body, which was usually his first warning of the **ketoacidosis**. What on earth was this all about? This was something new! CJ stayed with me for most of the day, and when he left to go home, he made me promise I would call him if things got worse. Charl had told CJ that if my ketone readings went as high as 3, he should take me to the hospital.

Well, my ketones continued to increase, and eventually the reading was 4.9. By the time that happened, the vomiting seemed to have gone away already, and I felt well. I couldn't believe that I was walking around the house when I knew that with a reading that high, I should have been in the hospital and on the drip. The fact that I was able to stomach fluids, except water, was a complete mystery to me. In all the years I have suffered from **ketoacidosis**, readings of 2.5 always had me hospitalised.

I had to cancel two appointments with friends that weekend, as I felt safer just being at home and not outdoors. I thought that even though I felt okay, I should rest my body, which I think was probably a very good thing to do. It took a whole week for me to get completely well, but this was the first time in my medical diabetic history that I did not end up going to the hospital when I had **ketoacidosis**. I can't help but wonder if my body has built up a resistance to the level of ketones that usually almost destroy me. It's so important to always listen to your body.

I now see an amazing diabetic specialist who has taught me something I have never known about before. I used to take the amount of fast-acting insulin that was required to carry me through a meal, and if I felt like eating something else about an hour or so after the meal, I would then have another injection of fast-acting insulin to carry me through whatever it was I had eaten then. My specialist told me there is a word for that. It is called stacking. That means that when I injected insulin into my body and then added more shortly after that, it stacked up in my system. I have since noticed that when I take an injection before meals and check it two hours after that, the blood sugar level will usually drop even though it goes up at first. In the past, I would have given myself a correction injection, but now I won't inject again until before I eat my next main meal. Before breakfast, lunch, dinner, and bedtime are the only times I will inject the fast-acting insulin into my body, and at bedtime, I will only give myself one or two units maximum if it is needed. I have noticed that with eating correctly, there is never any need for me to inject before going to bed.

One evening, while we were outside, Charl was working on our horse's new stable, and I was just about to rug him up for the night when I felt my sugar level dropping. All the normal feelings were there. I felt the numbness in my head and felt sleepy and weak, but unlike my usual way, when I act immediately to get my sugar level up again, I chose to carry on working with Bobby for just a little bit longer before I decided to go into the house to get something sugary into my system. That was a very big mistake! I had let the low go too far. I told Charl I needed sugar but did not come across as being too concerned, so he carried on doing the job he was busy with, while I made my way up the stairs and into the house.

Once I was inside, I opened up the freezer and reached in for the ice cream tub. I do have to say I had been doing clean eating for approximately a month, so when I put the first spoon of ice cream into my mouth, it woke up all my taste buds; they were having a party! The sweet taste was amazing, and so instead of only having two or three tablespoons, I started gulping the ice cream down. It was delicious! After a while, I realised I had better stop; otherwise, I would end up eating the entire tub, or what was left of it. Then I reached for the cookie jar instead.

The cookies went down very well too, and after eating a lot of them, I went to the pantry and opened up a packet of liquorice and ate several pieces of that as well.

As you can imagine, after having had such a big sugar binge, **BAM-CFS!!!!!** I was worried my sugar level would go in the opposite direction and would end up being sky-high. I bet you can guess what is coming next. I reached out for the fast-acting insulin pen, loaded it, and injected about seven units into my body. After all that had happened, I felt okay to go downstairs to carry on with other jobs that had to be done.

That night, I cooked a rather fatty, high-carbohydrates meal. **BAM-CFS!!!!!** That is something I don't like to do, but every now and then, it does happen. I fried chops and onions, and I also fried potato cakes; then just to top it all off, I added fried eggs too. We also had bread rolls with margarine. I enjoyed every mouthful; however, while I was busy eating my dinner, I couldn't help but feel guilty, so straight after the meal, I gave myself another fast-acting insulin shot. I injected about twenty units into my body. After cleaning up the kitchen and having a shower, I hopped into bed to watch a movie on TV before turning out the light and going to sleep.

Just before midnight, I woke up to the most terrifying feeling. Whenever I have had a sugar low in my sleep, I have always had the same dream, and in the dream, I am constantly struggling with the low blood sugar that won't go away. I was woken up to Charl talking to me and telling me to sit up in the bed. I could clearly hear him, but I was afraid to move because I thought I would end up dying. I seemed to have passed the danger level of passing away in the dream, and I managed to sit up in the bed. Charl told me I was having a low, and he was trying to get me to drink some fruit juice. I started sipping on the juice and then realised how saturated with sweat I was. Charl changed my pajamas and put a T-shirt on me. While this was all going on, I got a craving for soup. He went to the kitchen and made me one of those instant soups, which I was looking forward to drinking. As soon as I sipped on that, I felt nauseous and couldn't finish it. Charl gave me a soft drink as well, and I eventually felt myself stabilising again.

Because Charl has lived with my diabetes for such a long time, he is very clued-up on what to do if it gets the better of me, and thank God literally that he does. This went on until 3 a.m. I eventually felt quite well again, and we went back to sleep.

Charl kept a record of what time this started happening, and he also kept a record of my sugar readings during the three hours it took him to deal with me. I explained to him what had happened earlier on that evening, and then it all made sense to him why this had happened. The insulin had been stacking in my body.

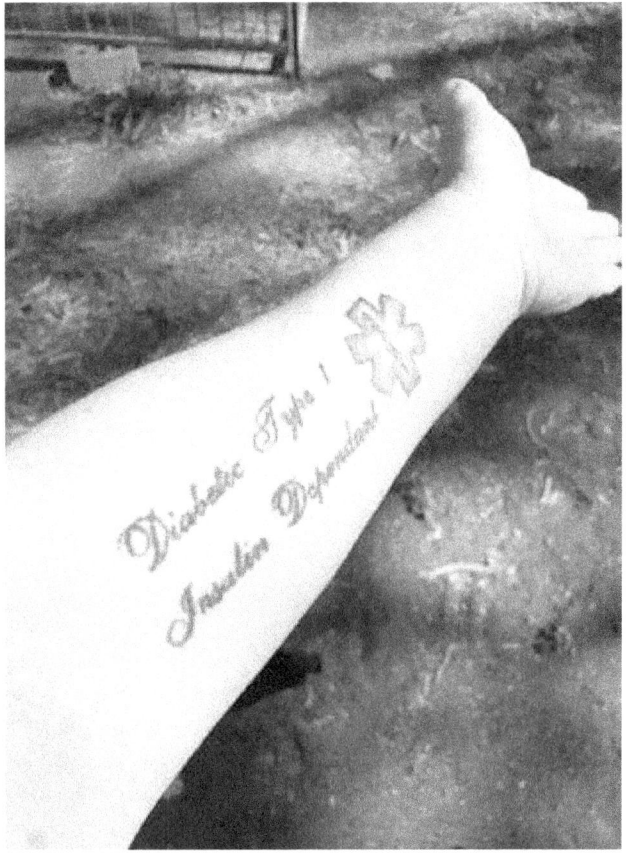

SURPRISE!

This is my arm everyone! I just want to say that as you all will know, we have to be cautious about certain things that can lead to infections in our bodies. Before I had the tattoo, I thought about the chance that I could be taking, but then I also thought about the good that it could do for me if I ever fainted or ended up in a car accident. I pictured myself lying on the ground, unconscious, and nobody being aware of my health condition. But, if I wore the tattoo on my arm where it would be noticeable, it could end up saving my life, for example, if somebody called an ambulance, the paramedics would be instantly aware of what they would have to deal with before they even got to where I was laying down on the ground.

I love the bracelets and necklaces that are made for us, but for me there is probably less chance of my arm disappearing and getting lost somewhere.

This is just a personal choice. We all have different preferences, and I really hope you enjoy mine.

CHAPTER 16

A FEW HANDY HINTS

- A few years ago, one of my jobs was being a cleaner. I used to work at one of the local police stations. One morning, whilst I was having a conversation with one of the police officers, the topic of diabetes came up. He asked me why I wasn't wearing a medic alert bracelet. I told him I found that it got in my way and that it also didn't match the jewellery I wore when going out. He came up with such a brilliant idea. He suggested it might be a good idea to have a tattoo on my arm that indicated I am a diabetic. I didn't waste any time, and within the next few days, I had the tattoo done. I didn't want it to stand out as such, so I had it done on the inside of my left arm.

- I have experienced using the various gadgets that are available to do blood sugar monitoring that gave me a reading without having to prick my finger. I found that very useful, because all I had to do was swipe the monitor over the shell that was inserted into my arm. That was all good and well, but I found that I sometimes knocked the shell out of my arm when walking past door frames. I just had to be very cautious when I wore it.

- I also used a different monitor wherein the shell was inserted into my stomach. I found that one to be very annoying. The monitor would beep when my blood sugars were either too high or too low, and also when the monitor was out of range of the shell. It reminded me of having a small baby screaming all the time to be fed or changed. It was a brilliant gadget though. I never had to check my blood. It did that for me.

- The one thing I did come to realise is that I should have done some research on the different monitors that are available—and there are many—before purchasing any of them. They are very expensive; however, the range to choose from is big, and they are well worth every penny spent.

- During Cyclone Marcia, we lost power for nine days. It was the first time Charl and I had lived through something like that. It was a huge wake-up call, because I had a lot of insulin stored in the fridge and no way of keeping it cool. Fortunately, one of our neighbours had a generator and was kind enough to let me keep the insulin in their fridge. We have since then bought ourselves a generator, so there is no need to be worried about power outages in the future.

- I have always been very conscious of cuts and scratches, as you should be as a diabetic. Every time I get a scratch from our dogs, or anything else, I am inclined to use an alcohol swab to disinfect it. Infection seems to take longer to heal in a diabetic, as opposed to a non-diabetic. The feet seem to be more susceptible to infections if not cared for. I know someone who is a prime example of this. He had a blister on one of his toes and ignored it. The result was him getting gangrene in his foot, which resulted in his leg being amputated from the knee down. Later on down the track, he ended up losing his other leg as well. This, however, is also common knowledge.

- I always used to use sweeteners as a substitute for sugar. For many years, I thought I was doing myself a favour, but I have since learnt that I am better off not using them at all. I noticed I was suffering from memory loss, which was very worrying. After doing a bit of research, I learnt that some of the ingredients in certain sweeteners can result in memory loss.

- Before I leave my house to go to town or anywhere else, I always check my little bag that contains all my insulin, needles, etc. to make sure there is enough of everything to last me for the day.

One day, though, I did not do this. I must have been in a hurry, because when I got to town and was ready to have lunch with a friend, I discovered that I did not have my diabetic bag with me. I needed to take insulin before eating my lunch, so I quickly hurried off to the pharmacy that was in the shopping complex. I had handed in many prescriptions for insulin in the past at that pharmacy, so I thought they would be understanding of my circumstance and would let me buy an insulin pen from them. I was shocked when the lady behind the till told me, after checking with the pharmacist, that they would not supply me with a single insulin pen to get me through the day in town. I explained to them that I lived out of town, so it wasn't easy for me to go home to fetch my own insulin pen. She then told me that the pharmacist said I needed to make an appointment to see my doctor so that I could get a prescription from her, which would allow them to supply me with the insulin. Did the pharmacist not realise the urgency of me needing to have the insulin? If they insisted on me handing in a prescription (I did not need to ask the doctor for one, as I had a whole lot of insulin in the fridge at home), they could have given me the insulin and told me to come back to them later on that day if possible, or the next day, and hand it to them.

A similar thing happened after that, but the situation was handled differently. When I was in South Africa at the airport and was waiting to board an aeroplane to fly back to Australia, I realised I had left all my insulin in the fridge at my sister's house. Fortunately, there was a pharmacy at the airport, and when my sister Benita told the pharmacist of the situation I was in, he, without hesitation, handed me a fast-acting insulin pen. All I had to do was produce my diabetic card and pay for the insulin, and I walked away feeling very satisfied and had peace of mind that I would be able to use that pen on the trip back to Australia.

SUMMARY

To summarise, I would just like to say that I hope you have enjoyed my story.

I hope too that some of the events I have had to deal with will be of help to you. You might feel alone at times, but after you read this book, I hope you feel comfort in knowing that whatever you are experiencing as a diabetic is being experienced by others as well.

A very big thank you to my husband, Charl, who has stood by me from the very beginning up until now. He has literally been my lifesaver on more than one occasion.

I would also like to thank my two beautiful children, Charl Jnr and Carrin, for walking this very long path with me. As children, this could have been quite a traumatic event for them to have to witness, but with us educating them, they were able to deal with it and have been there to help me on so many occasions, some of which were life-threatening. My family have been and still are my rock, with all the love, care, concern, and support that they continuously show me every single day. I could never have survived for so long without them. A huge thank you too to the specialists, doctors, nurses, and diabetic educators and pathologists who have been involved with me along the way. As the patient, I felt irritable whilst lying in the various hospital beds, but I am very grateful for all the work and effort the medical staff put into taking care of me throughout the years.

Diabetes will always be a part of my everyday living. I will never be free from it, but I am so fortunate to have come this far and have learnt so much about the disease.

To my friends, I thank you for all your support, love, and care.

To my readers, I thank you for your interest in my story, and I hope I have given you something to relate to along the way. Look after yourselves. It's the only body you will ever have.

Thank you.

Celeste Barnard

INDEX

A

Allison (sister) 34-9, 68-70

Australia 5, 8, 34, 38, 40, 43-9, 51, 67, 70, 131-2

Australian consulate 42

B

Benita (sister) 69-70

Benjamin (dog) 9, 45, 52

Bernie (niece) 69

blood sugar levels vii, 1, 6, 31, 42, 55-6, 72, 77-8, 83-5, 93, 95-6, 98-9, 103-4, 106, 109, 115, 117, 119, 124-5

Brisbane 34, 40, 64-5, 69-71

C

Cape Town 34, 36, 43, 67-8

Carrin (daughter) 7, 13, 71, 76, 92-3, 99, 103-4, 133

Charl (husband) 7-8, 10, 13-18, 20-2, 24-8, 30-1, 42, 48-53, 57, 59-62, 64-5, 67, 71, 73-6, 79, 81, 99-102, 122-3, 125-6, 133

Chez (best friend) 25-6, 30, 42, 46-7

CJ (son) 7, 13, 71, 103, 123, 133

D

diabetes x-xi, 2-3, 5, 7-8, 11, 21, 29, 33, 54, 63, 72-3, 83-5, 87, 89-95, 97, 106, 108-10, 112, 116, 118-19, 121, 126, 134

diabetic educator 56, 60-1, 76, 114, 124, 133

Drake (doctor) 20-1, 30

Dubai 66-7, 70

I

insulin   vii, 9, 29-30, 52, 54-5, 63, 70, 77, 83-5, 91, 93-4, 96, 99-101, 106, 109, 115, 126, 130-2

  fast-acting   124

  long-acting   96-7

  short-acting   96, 114

intensive care unit (ICU)   35, 57-8, 60, 66

J

Johan (brother)   69

K

ketoacidosis   11, 49, 54, 63, 65, 67, 76, 88-9, 116, 122-4

ketones   54, 61, 65, 71, 75-6, 89, 107, 116, 122-4

Kuala Lumpur   39, 48, 50-1

M

Malaysia   34, 39, 41-2, 49-50, 61

P

Pat (sister)   34, 39, 69-70

R

Rocky (dog)   45

S

Sean (nephew)   36-7, 69

South Africa   viii, 7, 34-5, 38, 43, 50, 64-5, 70-1, 73, 82-3, 131

sporting activities   56, 89-94, 117

Z

Zimbabwe   7-8

www.ingramcontent.com/pod-product-compliance
Lightning Source LLC
Chambersburg PA
CBHW052051070526
44584CB00017B/2132